YOU CAN'T SAY THAT

Writers for Young People
Talk About Censorship, Free Expression,
and the Stories They Have to Tell

COMPILED AND EDITED BY
LEONARD S. MARCUS

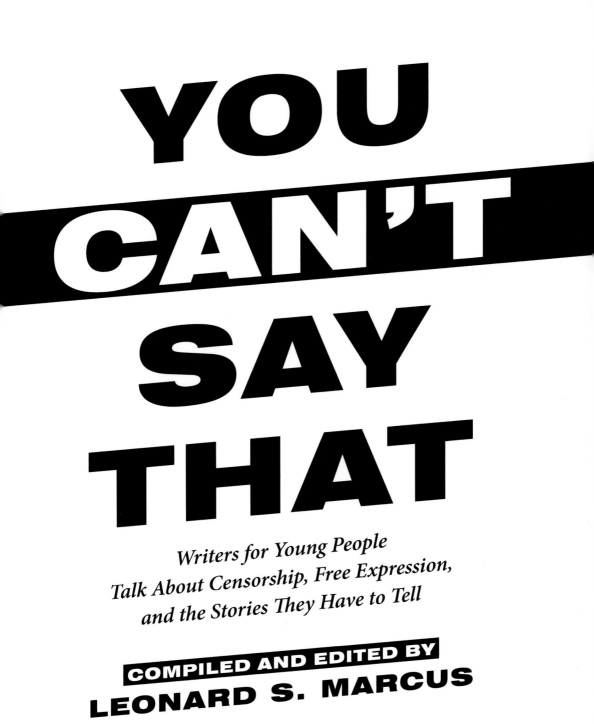

CANDLEWICK PRESS

First edition 2021

Library of Congress Catalog Card Number pending
ISBN 978-0-7636-9036-6

21 22 23 24 25 26 CCP 10 9 8 7 6 5 4 3 2 1

Printed in Shenzhen, Guangdong, China

This book was typeset in Minion Pro.

Candlewick Press
99 Dover Street
Somerville, Massachusetts 02144

www.candlewick.com

FOR MY UNCLE
ABE FREEDMAN,
who owned one of the first copies
of *Ulysses* to reach New York
and who always said
what he pleased

IN MEMORY

#

INTRODUCTION

censor: to examine in order to suppress or
delete anything considered objectionable
> —*Merriam-Webster's Collegiate Dictionary*

It's hard being a person.
We all know that.
> —from "Runaway Teen" by William Stafford

At the age of ten, it thrilled me to learn that history had once been made in Mount Vernon, New York, the quiet, tree-lined suburban town where my parents had chosen to raise their family. Quiet it was, with an imposing Carnegie library, an annual Fourth of July parade, one ten-story "skyscraper," and a place to grab a twenty-five-cent slice after school among the highlights. Back in pre–Revolutionary War times, though—the 1730s to be exact—Mount Vernon had been the site of real fireworks when a fearless newspaper publisher and journalist named John Peter Zenger dared to expose the assorted crimes of New York Colony's corrupt royal governor William Cosby, among them an attempt to fix a local election in which Mount Vernon's St. Paul's Church played a pivotal role. Enraged by the bad press, the governor had jailed Zenger, claiming his fiery verbal attacks were unlawful. At trial, the judge and jury disagreed with Cosby, and the charges against Zenger were dropped on the grounds that to publish the truth could never be a crime. In 1789, the Founding Fathers cited the Zenger case as they drafted the First

Amendment to the United States Constitution, a sweeping statement of principles that guaranteed citizens freedom of speech, of the press, and of religion and assembly, and the right to criticize their government. Ever since then, the First Amendment has stood as a shield protecting a wide swath of the basic rights that we as Americans enjoy, including the freedom to read and write whatever we please. As such, it has also served as a powerful safeguard against efforts at censorship, including those aimed at books for children and teens.

I can still recall the pride with which my fourth-grade teacher spoke to us about the Zenger trial, the First Amendment, and their long-term consequences. Thanks to the Founding Fathers' foresight and wisdom, she said, Americans had won the battle for freedom of expression. Lucky us for being the heirs to that noble legacy!

As I later realized, the story of that battle was far more complex, and far from over; attempts to censor the printed (and spoken) word have been a recurring feature of American history. In 1821, the Massachusetts Supreme Judicial Court banned the sale of a spicy English novel called *Fanny Hill* as an imminent threat to public morality. In 1873, Congress passed the Comstock Act, which, by making it illegal to send printed items ranging from erotica to birth control manuals through the mail, effectively denied access to these materials to millions of readers. Anthony Comstock, the bombastic moralist whose New York Society for the Suppression of Vice had vigorously lobbied for the legislation, next took aim at a type of sensational adventure fiction then attracting legions of teenage readers. Fans of "dime novels" purchased the spellbinding paperbacks at newsstands with their own pocket money and could not get enough of them. Comstock, however, certain the books were a corrupting influence, warned parents that, "[If] read before the intellect is quickened or judgment matured sufficient to show the harm of dwelling on these things, [then dime novels will] educate our youth in all the odious features of crime." Once again turning the postal system to his advantage, he managed to have the publishers' second-class-postage permits revoked, thereby sending their shipping costs skyrocketing. Comstock was a self-righteous bully on a mission to impose his own morals on everyone. Imagine what damage he might have done in the age of Twitter.

At the same time that Comstock was waging war against an entire genre of popular teen fiction, one of America's most highly regarded authors, Mark Twain, found himself in the censors' crosshairs when the trustees of the Concord (Massachusetts) public library voted to ban *Adventures of Huckleberry Finn* from its shelves. "Coarseness" of language was the scornful complaint, along with the Olympian judgment that Twain's book was "trash and suitable only for the slums." The author gamely shrugged off the criticisms with the prediction that sales would soar on the news of the novel's spectacular notoriety.

While Twain in the long run had nothing to fear from the censors, he lived to see *Adventures of Huckleberry Finn* banned at the Denver, Omaha, and Brooklyn public libraries, among others. His book remained a cultural lightning rod, not least because, in the guise of a picaresque adventure story told by a rascally teenager, he had written a powerful meditation on racism in America. In later years, critics tended to miss this point altogether and to zero in on Twain's repeated use of the word *nigger* instead as proof that the novel had in fact been written from a racist point of view. Among the objectors, ironically, was the principal of the Mark Twain Intermediate School, in Fairfax, Virginia, whose initial attempt to restrict student access to *Adventures of Huckleberry Finn* was set aside in favor of a thoughtful plan to provide students with the historical context they would need to understand Twain's exquisitely nuanced, funny-serious book.

In the long history of censorship, Anthony Comstock rates as a comparative latecomer. Two millennia before, the Greek philosopher Plato had boldly laid out the case for censorship as a legitimate exercise of government's moral authority: "The poet," he declared, "shall compose nothing contrary to the ideas of the lawful, or just, or beautiful, or good, which are allowed in the state; nor shall he be permitted to communicate his compositions to any private individual, until he shall have shown them to the appointed censors and the guardians of the law, and they are satisfied with them." Plato's own teacher, Socrates, had been sentenced to death in democratic Athens for worshipping false gods and planting dangerous ideas in the minds of the city-state's youth. By then, in the Roman Republic, high government officials called *censores*—the origin of our term—not only conducted the census but were also charged with regulating the moral behavior of those they entered into the rolls. Citing early examples like these, historian Arthur Schlesinger Jr. wrote that the persistence of censorship into our time should surprise no one: "The instinct to suppress discomforting ideas," Schlesinger observed, "is rooted deep in human nature. It is rooted above all in profound human propensities to faith and to fear."

By the year I turned eight, two major instances of censorship of young people's reading material had already occurred within my lifetime. First, in 1954, a psychiatrist named Fredric Wertham published a popular study in which he blamed the rise of juvenile delinquency in America on the bad influence of horror comics like *Tales from the Crypt*. The alarm Wertham sounded in his book *Seduction of the Innocent* generated enough public concern to trigger a full-dress Senate investigation. Guided by fear of further government meddling, the comics publishers huddled among themselves and voluntarily came up with a plan to censor their own industry. The Comics Code Authority satisfied the senators and dampened the creative spirits of comics artists and writers for years afterward.

Then, four years later, Garth Williams's picture book *The Rabbits' Wedding* stirred outrage in Alabama, drawing public condemnation in the state legislature and the press. Williams insisted his tale about two rabbits—one white, the other black—who fall in love and marry was nothing more than a tender love story for four-year-olds. But in the segregationist South, some readers interpreted the book as a sinister endorsement of interracial marriage. In response to the outcry, *The Rabbits' Wedding* was pulled from the Alabama State Library's circulating collection and the state librarian resigned her post.

By then, librarians had begun to see the protection of readers' and writers' First Amendment rights as fundamental to their mission. In 1967, the American Library Association took the historic step of establishing the Office for Intellectual Freedom (OIF) as a permanent first line of defense against efforts to limit public access to books and other library materials. Because in the United States nearly all censorship attempts originate not with the government in Washington but rather with a challenge by a private individual or group at the local or state level, a reasonable, law-based, community-centered process for resolving far-flung disputes over book access was urgently needed. The OIF proceeded to propose guidelines for libraries and schools to use in developing such a process for their own locality, and to publish the *Intellectual Freedom Manual* and other reference materials of value to anyone facing a challenge.

Not all librarians understood their role in the same way. The depiction of a naked child in Maurice Sendak's *In the Night Kitchen*, a 1971 Caldecott Honor winner, prompted a staff member at the Caldwell Parish (Louisiana) Library, according to a local press report that was reprinted in *School Library Journal*, to respond by "diapering the little boys [*sic*] with white tempera paint." In a press release dated June 9, 1972, the publisher, Harper & Row, characterized the report as "representative of several . . . that have come out of public and school libraries throughout the country." The release quoted in full a statement that Ursula Nordstrom, publisher of Harper Junior Books, had recently sent to 380 librarians, authors, artists, academics, and fellow publishers in which she condemned the alteration of *In the Night Kitchen* and solicited their support. "At first," Nordstrom wrote, "the thought of librarians painting diapers or pants on the naked hero of Sendak's book might seem amusing, merely a harmless eccentricity on the part of some prim few. On reconsideration, however, this behavior should be recognized for what it is: an act of censorship by mutilation rather than by obvious suppression." Harper received a total of 425 endorsements of Nordstrom's eloquent plea to "preserv[e] the First Amendment freedoms for everyone involved in the processes of communicating ideas."

In 1982, a sharp uptick in book challenges led booksellers to adopt an activist stance, too. That year's American Booksellers Association's

annual trade show featured a prominent display of five hundred challenged titles stacked high in a locked cage, with an overhead sign "warning" that some people considered the books "dangerous." To raise public awareness, the booksellers teamed up with the OIF's Judith Krug and the National Association of College Stores to launch Banned Books Week as an annual national observance.

To further inform the public, since 1990, the OIF has compiled an annual list of the year's ten most frequently challenged books. Year after year, books for children and teens have dominated the OIF list, sharing space with a seemingly random assortment of other works, including Aldous Huxley's *Brave New World*, John Steinbeck's *Of Mice and Men*, and the Bible. The lists have the value of an attention-grabbing, public-awareness tool, but as the OIF has noted, they do not tell the whole story, due to the fact that the majority of book challenges each year are assumed to go unreported. A major reason for this underreporting is local book defenders' fear of further inflaming an already emotionally charged situation. A recurring theme in the conversations that follow is the personal cost that librarians, teachers, and others who rise to the defense of a challenged book often pay for their efforts: a cost measured in emotional stress, ostracism by opposing community members, and even loss of employment. These human costs tend to remain hidden from public view, as does the pressure (subtle or not) that a librarian or other defender who has withstood a challenge may feel the next time a potentially controversial book comes up for purchase, as well as the pressure to self-censor (also subtle or not) that an author or publisher may experience, knowing that an earlier book prompted a trouble-ridden or painful incident.

The impulse to censor may indeed be too deeply ingrained in human nature to ever die out altogether, but the intensity with which it is acted upon ebbs and flows in sync with changes in society, especially a society's shifting hopes and fears. Judy Blume recalls the 1970s, the decade in which she published her first fourteen smart, funny, daringly outspoken chapter books and novels, as a "good decade for writers and readers." Then:

> Almost overnight, following the presidential election of 1980, the censors crawled out of the woodwork, organized and determined. . . . Those who were most active in trying to ban books came from the "religious right" but the impulse spread like a contagious disease. Other parents, confused and uncertain, were happy to jump on the bandwagon. Book banning satisfied their need to feel in control of their children's lives.

As efforts to ban or remove books by Blume and others from school and library shelves accelerated, a landmark United States Supreme Court decision, *Board of Education, Island Trees Union Free School District No. 26 v. Pico* (1982), amplified school students' First Amendment rights as readers. The case centered on an attempt by a suburban New York school board to withdraw from its high school and junior high school library shelves eleven books that it considered objectionable. In a narrow 5–4 decision, the high court ruled that the board did not have the right to deny students access to books merely because it disapproved of the ideas expressed in them.

Blume herself became an ardent spokesperson on behalf of freedom of expression, often appearing at public events with Madeleine L'Engle, whose novel *A Wrinkle in Time* was sharply criticized by some readers for being too Christian (because of its references to Jesus and guardian angels), and by others for not being Christian enough (because it seemed to place Jesus on an equal footing with secular visionaries like Einstein and Beethoven and to validate witchcraft). Activists like Blume and L'Engle found they did not have to act alone. In addition to the Office for Intellectual Freedom, other nonprofit organizations such as the Freedom to Read Foundation, the National Coalition Against Censorship, PEN America Center, the Authors Guild, and the Comic Book Legal Defense Fund were there to provide both legal and moral support to authors, illustrators, librarians, teachers, and others whose First Amendment rights were under threat. The added impact and resources of an institutional response helped to level the playing field during the 1980s, when book challenges increasingly took the form of concerted efforts on the part of well-financed organizations including the conservative Moral Majority and Eagle Forum. Since then, pro–First Amendment advocacy groups have only grown in importance as American society has become ever more fractious politically and the Internet and new media have dramatically expanded both the universe of censorable material and the arsenal of weapons at the disposal of objectors from across the political spectrum who are intent on imposing their views on others.

The thirteen authors you are about to hear from have all published books that have been repeatedly targeted for removal or banning from school or library shelves. The objectors' concerns have tended to cluster around a small number of complex and emotionally fraught themes. Violence, race, sexuality, and gender identity have been major flash points. "Lack of moral tone" and "coarseness of language"—"Calling Mark Twain!"—are also frequently cited, as are drug use, suicide, and irreverence about religion.

Book challengers often justify their actions in the name of protecting children from what they consider to be premature exposure to information or knowledge of one kind or another. But people disagree about what protecting the young means as it relates to books. In fact, one of the most basic changes in books for young readers over the past half century has been a rethinking of this question, with most authors turning away from the goal of sheltering young people from a knowledge of the world's dangers and toward the very different (but not less caring) goal of preparing the young to live in the world in which they find themselves by forthrightly providing them with critical information and understanding. Maurice Sendak, Louise Fitzhugh, Robert Cormier, and Judy Blume are among the authors who led the way in creating books rooted in psychological realism and the assumption that young people are more knowing than the grown-up world has traditionally believed. However, with opinions so polarized about the underlying purpose of books for young readers, the likelihood of continued challenges and bans seems high.

Impassioned discussions about a controversial book—when they *are* discussions in which each side respects the rights of the other—are a healthy exercise of our First Amendment legacy. In the heat of a bitter book challenge, however, such good-faith dialogues do not always happen. In the interviews that follow, stories of an objector's refusal to engage in a frank and open discussion are many, but so, too, are stories of unsettled but thoughtful readers who were willing and able to change their minds.

Here, then, from thirteen accomplished authors for young people are fresh perspectives on why writers write their books in the way they choose, regardless of the consequences; and on what can happen to a book once the author lets go of it and it enters the public square of our country and world's wildly divergent panoply of ideals, beliefs, and expectations.

Here, too, is a chance to examine at close range what it means when any person or group, however well intentioned, seeks to limit the writing or reading lives of others. Supreme Court justice Potter Stewart got to the heart of this question when he wrote:

Censorship reflects a society's lack of confidence in itself. It is a hallmark of an authoritarian regime. Long ago those who wrote our First Amendment charted a different course. They believed a society can be truly strong only when it is truly free. . . . A book worthless to me may convey some value to my neighbor. In the free society to which our Constitution has committed us, it is for each to choose for himself.

MATT DE LA PEÑA
Born 1973, National City, California

Matt de la Peña grew up in a mixed-race family in Southern California, the son of a Mexican American father and a white mom. During childhood car trips to visit his Mexican relatives, he had his first glimpses of the US-Mexican border and began to reflect on its meaning and on what sometimes felt like his own divided life. In high school, de la Peña turned to writing poetry—secretly at first while also making a more socially acceptable mark as a basketball player, or "half-Mexican hoop head," as he later described himself. Poetry became a private back channel for connecting with his tangled legacy as a "Mexican white boy."

For de la Peña, as the first member of his family to attend college, heading off to the University of the Pacific initially felt like an incursion into alien territory. College life soon came to mean something quite different, however: the freedom to write poetry and fiction in the open, and to do so with the realistic expectation of finding an appreciative audience. Being accepted in this way was a life-changing experience.

De la Peña never consciously set out to be a teen fiction author, but he found himself drawn to telling stories about young people like the one he had once been: "self-defined nonreaders who spend all day reading the world." He never planned to write controversial books, either. But his keenness to explore uncomfortable questions relating to class and race in America and to do so in a raw, culturally specific street vernacular, made some pushback all but inevitable. When the objections to his books came, they brought him into closer contact with his readers.

As de la Peña explains in our interview, turning to picture-book writing represented more to him than a break from the marathon effort required to craft a fully realized novel. It also marked his return to writing poetry. He received the 2016 Newbery Medal for *Last Stop on Market Street*, a picture book with illustrations by Christian Robinson that reads like a lyric poem.

De la Peña and I met as fellow speakers at the Bank Street College of Education's 2016 conference titled "Who Are You to Say? Children's Literature and the Censorship Conversation." We recorded this conversation in my downtown Brooklyn office three years later, not long before he moved back with his family to the Southern California city where he was born and has set so many of his stories.

———

LEONARD S. MARCUS: *In your books, you are interested in boundaries: the border that separates Mexico and the United States, the line between poetry and prose, the fine line between the person who is your friend and the one who might be your enemy.*

MATT DE LA PEÑA: My dad's family came from Mexico to live in California. They crossed the border and landed in San Diego just before he was born. I grew up right next to the Mexican border in what was considered a bad neighborhood. It fascinated me that people in San Diego would refer to us as poor, but the minute we crossed the border into Mexico to see my grandfather, we would be considered wealthy by the community there. I thought a lot about the fact that that arbitrary border seemed to change who I was depending on which side I was on.

My dad had several brothers and sisters, and his mother, my Mexican grandmother, was our matriarch. I remember one time when I was about twelve, she was with us as we were crossing back into the US, and there were these kids banging on our car window, trying to sell us gum. She looked at me and said, "Just so you know, Matt. We have Spanish in us, too. We're not *just* Mexican." It was a huge moment, as I realized she was ashamed of a part of her background. She was mostly referring to class.

LSM: *How well did you know Spanish then?*

MDLP: I grew up around Spanish and could understand most of what was being said, but my Spanish was never good enough for me to speak the language. Back then, a lot of Mexican fathers didn't want their kids to speak Spanish. We were to be "American." I guess my dad's biggest regret right now is that he didn't teach his kids Spanish. He was always a very quiet man, so even if he hadn't discouraged us, we probably wouldn't have become Spanish speakers. I've heard somewhere that you end up speaking the language of your mother. For me that fits, because my mom was with us the whole time. She was the one talking to us, tucking us in, reading us stories. My dad was out working, and when he came home, he was very quiet because he was tired from having worked so hard.

LSM: *Were you, like your character Danny in your second novel* Mexican WhiteBoy, *driven into silence because of your limited Spanish?*

MDLP: Yes, Danny came out of my personal experience. My mom had no family, so the only family we knew was the Mexican side. Because I was the lightest of all my family members, I felt "less than" in some ways in relation to my cousins and uncles. And yet my grandmother saw me as the "chosen one"—because I was the lightest.

There was so much complexity around skin color and about where you fit along the Mexican American spectrum. When I wrote *Mexican WhiteBoy*, the greatest mistake I made in the first draft was judging Danny by saying in effect, "You're not Mexican enough. You didn't fully embrace who you are and respect your family." When I reread the first draft, I thought, *Why isn't this working?*—and I realized that it wasn't my job to judge Danny. I had to pull back and let readers have space to decide about Danny for themselves.

LSM: *Danny feels guilty about being better educated than the people around him. Like him, you were the first member of your family to go to college.*

MDLP: My family thought it was a great thing that I was going to college. When I got there, though, I was shocked by how much guilt I felt. You know, real life is still happening back home, and I'm going off to fraternity parties and to basketball games surrounded by cheering fans. But for the first time in my life, I also felt recognized not just as a member of my family but as me. I asked myself, *Why am I feeling like a sell-out for succeeding?* I was at a private college where I was confronted for the first time by extreme wealth—kids driving Mercedes on campus! I asked myself, *What do I think of this? How do I deal with this?* I had a very complicated reaction, which I later explored in *Mexican WhiteBoy*. On the basketball team, we were all from poor families, so I was lucky because I had the basketball community as well as college counselors to support me, and within six months I had begun to feel that being at college was an amazing thing.

LSM: *What kind of a child were you?*

MDLP: Quiet, introspective. Quiet like my dad. I always describe my dad as an "artist with no art," because he saw the world slant but had no way to express it. Art was the furthest thing from his mind as he worked at low-level jobs to help us survive.

I was also a basketball nerd. Summers, I would play basketball sunup to sundown. I studied the world of pickup basketball, which provided me with almost another family. My first book, *Ball Don't*

Lie, is really about a nontraditional family. Here are these guys. They're selling drugs. They're working at gas stations. But they're my family while we're playing together all summer. Maybe they aren't the "best" people to learn from, but you do learn about a certain part of the world that way.

LSM: *Uno's father, Senior [in* Ball Don't Lie*], is such an incredible talker. I suppose you could say that his wild monologues are his art.*

MDLP: I love that character. I'm fascinated by parental figures who say things that are wrong but present them in a wise way. When I was writing about Senior, I thought, *What's more important: A dad who has all the correct answers or a dad who is there for his son, a dad who is present?*

LSM: *Were you a reader as a child?*

MDLP: No. There were just a few books I liked. One was Sandra Cisneros's *The House on Mango Street,* which I read probably fifteen times. I was reluctant to explore most other books. When we read *The Catcher in the Rye* in high school, I couldn't connect with it. I remember thinking, *Why is this rich kid whining?* I read *Catcher* many years later and found so much more in it. I was the chip-on-the-shoulder kid, and I rejected any book about what upper-class life was like. Looking back, I think I wore poverty as a badge of honor.

LSM: *Like you, your character Miguel in* We Are Here *changes his mind about* Catcher in the Rye.

MDLP: He did it a lot quicker than I did!

LSM: *Why are you so drawn to writing about teen characters?*

MDLP: I read some Walter Dean Myers and Gary Soto when I was young, and I remember thinking then that there was something special about the coming-of-age moment. When I was getting an MFA in a program for writers of adult fiction, I was already writing in the teen voice, even though I had never heard of YA as a genre. It was only when my first book was bought by a publisher as a YA novel that I realized I was writing YA.

LSM: *How does writing a picture book compare with writing a novel?*

MDLP: Turning to picture books was like going home, because all through high school, I had been writing poetry, and a picture-book text is like a poem in many ways. I was writing poems about being biracial, poems about Mexico and about my family, and I would show them to no one, because I didn't think that writing poetry was what a boy was supposed to be doing. I kept it quiet! One of the benefits of going to college is that you find a community that is more welcoming to your being a sensitive thinker. I had professors at college who were hungry for the poetry I was writing. Now when I write a picture book, it's like going back to that good time, when I was first moved to express myself.

LSM: Mexican WhiteBoy *got caught up in controversy in Tucson, Arizona, in 2012. What happened there?*

MDLP: It started with an email from a girl who wrote, "I love your book. You should come to my high school." She was a Mexican girl, as I could tell by her name. I forgot about this, but then the girl's school librarian invited me to visit the school and worked out all the arrangements. Next, an email came from a teacher at the same school, who said that my book had just been banned from their school and asked what she could do about it. I thought, *Whoa!* I had never had a book banned and did not really know what that meant. I had no idea what to do. At first, I just wrote back and said I was sorry to hear about it. Then I received a rundown of exactly what was happening. The Mexican American Studies Program in the Tucson public school system was being challenged by people in power in Tucson. The immediate reason for this was that somebody from the program had made the statement at a Mexican American event that "Republicans hate Mexicans."

After that, the books that were being taught as part of the program became caught up in a political struggle. Republicans with the power to do so proceeded to dismantle the program and banned the books associated with it from the public schools. The symbolism of what followed was pretty powerful. In one schoolroom where the students were reading *Mexican WhiteBoy*, the superintendent's staff came into the classroom and literally took the kids' copies of my book out of their hands, put the books in a box labeled BANNED, and took them down to the basement. I remember hearing about this and thinking, *Oh, my God!* The idea of the program, which had been highly effective, was to motivate Mexican children to learn by giving them books to read by people with last names like their own and featuring characters like them.

A book in which I had explored my own identity had now become part of this political back-and-forth.

I did end up visiting that high school, and when I got there, I saw that the closing of the program had actually further motivated the Mexican American kids. They had begun to fight for the program. At one point, they had even chained themselves to some desks in city hall. They were activists now.

That visit, which the savvy school librarian had managed to arrange without the superintendent or the principal knowing about it, was the most powerful experience I have ever had as an author. We talked before about my not having felt Mexican enough as a kid, and here I was, going to speak to the kids at a school that had had my book taken away from them because it was about being Mexican American. The students and I huddled together. It was as profound an experience for me as it was for them.

A reporter from the *New York Times* who had heard about the controversy had come along with me to Tucson. Some of the students joined us for dinner the night before the event. I loved watching these supposedly "at-risk" kids being interviewed by the *New York Times* and sharing a taco. It was all pretty amazing.

LSM: *The Mexican American Studies Program was eventually reinstated, wasn't it?*

MDLP: Yes, but at first it was reinstated in a way that was totally unsatisfactory. They allowed the program to resume but would not give course credit to the students who enrolled in it. That meant that students would have to take a second literature course as well.

Considering that these students were already struggling, it was unlikely they would want to do so. In 2019, the program had its accreditation restored. It took a long time.

LSM: *How did the Tucson experience affect you?*

MDLP: It made me understand the power of literature. It made me realize that a book is bigger than a book. A book can be in more places than I can ever be. Who knows what impact it might have?

LSM: *What do you suppose motivates people like those who tried to shut down Tucson's Mexican American Studies Program and who challenge and ban other books for young readers?*

MDLP: I imagine it's a combination of fear, concern for self-preservation, and often a loving impulse to protect their children. Obviously, most of the time I think that impulse is misguided.

LSM: *How do you go about imagining your characters?*

MDLP: The characters come first but without necessarily my knowing much of anything about them. For example, with *We Were Here,* I thought, *Here's Miguel and here's Rondell, like George and Lennie from John Steinbeck's* Of Mice and Men. But I didn't even know at first that Miguel and Rondell were going to break out of the group home where they were living. I had worked in a group home for a couple of years, and I knew I would write a book about that experience someday. Another character in the book, Mong, came out of nowhere. I had thought he would just be another one of the kids in

the group home, when all of a sudden Mong became the catalyst for them all to run away.

LSM: *I love that Miguel and the other runaways go right up to the Mexican border but at the last minute decide not to cross it.*

MDLP: I knew I wanted Miguel to get up to the border. When he does get there, he sees a boy on the other side who's just like him, and he asks himself the same question I once asked myself: *Why does that boy have so many fewer opportunities on his side of the border than I do on mine?* I wanted him to have that epiphany.

LSM: *Why did you decide that Mong would walk into the ocean and end his own life?*

MDLP: That was a heavy moment. I think of these three boys who had lost the right to control their lives and who wanted to reclaim some sort of control. Mong is very ill, so for him control means, *If I'm going to go, I want to be able to say when I go.* For Rondell, control has to do with religion. He wants to make sure that God can see him. Miguel just wants his mother to see him again. It was fun to watch them try to regain control over their lives, each in his own way.

Mong is a more peripheral character, and for most of the story, we know him through Miguel. But in the scene before he disappears, he talks about himself in a way that feels like he is talking directly to the reader. He is saying, *This is who I am.* Cormac McCarthy is my favorite writer. I read a couple of paragraphs from his novel *Suttree* every day before I write. What he's really good at doing is introducing you to a character right before he passes or disappears. As the reader, you feel that you are meeting that character before it's too late. And that's how it is with Mong.

LSM: *Mong starts out being such an appalling person, a violent kid capable of tearing other people apart. Later, though, he becomes a genuinely sympathetic character.*

MDLP: He's a reflection of the way I saw the kids at the group home. You meet these kids who grew up in places where they had to put up a front and assert themselves to other boys and men in order to get respect. Once they had that respect, then maybe they could reveal their humanity.

For kids like that, sometimes language is no longer about the meaning of the words. It's just about aggression. Sometimes real violence happens when they don't have the language to express how they feel. But the reverse can also happen. In *The House on Mango Street*, there is a vignette called "Darius & the Clouds." It's about this grubby kid. He's the mess-up, the kind of kid who, as Sandra Cisneros says, would touch a rat with a stick and chase girls with it. Suddenly, though, Darius looks up at the sky and says to his friends, "You all see that cloud, that fat one there? . . . That one next to the one that look like popcorn. . . . That's God." It's a moment of poetry. Sandra Cisneros gave him poetry. I think that's so beautiful, and it was a hugely influential moment for me.

LSM: *The freewheeling philosophical conversations between Miguel and Rondell in* We Were Here *and between Danny and Uno in* Mexican WhiteBoy *remind me of those in* Adventures of Huckleberry Finn *as Huck and Jim make their way down the river on their raft. Has Mark Twain meant a lot to you as a writer?*

MDLP: Absolutely. Especially for his voice. The fact that he owns the vernacular. It feels so free.

LSM: *In* Mexican WhiteBoy, *you say thank you to some people for help with the dialect. Why did you need that help?*

MDLP: I needed lots of help. The dialect is very specific to Southern California. Spanish slang in San Diego is different from Spanish slang in Texas. Both are way different from Spanish slang in New York. If you took a Dominican from New York and set him down in my neighborhood in San Diego, he'd understand the basic premise of what was being said but not the specifics. So two people I had gone to high school with and my dad all helped me get the slang right. It's a mix of hip-hop urban and Spanglish. It's the language of my childhood.

LSM: *James Joyce said, "In the particular is contained the universal." Is that why it was so important to you to get the slang right?*

MDLP: A hundred percent! I had a huge epiphany when I was in grad school. There was a fifty-year-old man in my writing class named Fernando. Before he got to our program, he had had a whole other life as a bus driver in Mexico City. We would go with him to this bar and be sitting there, drinking, and he would have us in the palm of his hands with his amazing stories about driving a bus in Mexico. Who got on and who got off the bus. Fights that took place. He was such a genius about pacing. He'd bring us right to the point of demanding, "Well, so, *then* what happened?" and he'd sit back, take a long sip from his drink, and shake his head as if he was thinking about it himself. We'd go, "Jesus Christ, tell us what happened!"

Then he'd bring a story he had written to class, and it would suck. Every time. We would think, *What's wrong with this guy? The best storyteller. Why can't he write a story?* Then one day the professor said, "Fernando, why is there no Spanish in this story?" Fernando said, "Oh, sir, I didn't think it was legal in America." "Come on," our teacher said back. "Any time you hear Spanish as you are writing, include it in the scene." The next story he turned in was just like sitting with him in the bar.

LSM: *Since we are talking about cultural authenticity in books, what do you think about Own Voices, the idea that writers should not attempt to portray the experiences of characters who are from outside their own cultural or social group?*

MDLP: I'm an advocate for Own Voices, but right now the conversation seems too black-and-white. How far do we take it? Someone could even say that you have to have been in a group home to write about a group home—not just as a counselor but as a resident. And I think we have to acknowledge that, within Own Voices, authors are sometimes fringe members of their group. I look at myself. I'm writing about the Mexican community, the border community, the mixed-race community. But I've always felt like a fringe member of it. Maybe my studying it and writing about it is my way of being more a part of it. Being on the fringes can be a good place to report from.

LSM: *Have any of your other books encountered trouble?*

MDLP: Of all my books, *Last Stop on Market Street* has received the most criticism—not formal challenges but a lot of email complaints. It's because of the language. I don't always use "proper" English, and some teachers of younger children have said, "We spend all this time trying to teach our young people how to speak correctly, and here's this book that has a wide reach and is showing them how to speak incorrectly." If you think about it, that's a coded racist response. I also think it shows that we don't give kids enough credit for understanding what is sometimes called code switching. That is, when that little boy is with his grandmother, he's in the safest place in the world, so he's going to speak the language of his grandmother. But I bet that when he goes to school, he's going to know the difference and speak the language of school.

In another picture book, *Love*, there was a suggestion of alcoholism in a scene in which two parents have been arguing, and a major bookstore chain said it would not carry the book unless we removed the reference. They said people in middle America would go into the store, see a picture book titled *Love*, and have certain positive expectations about the book. My publisher and I chose to keep the reference in anyway, and after *Love* did well with the indie booksellers, the big chain store came back with a substantial order, too. I was so surprised by all this, because I would have thought that if winning the Newbery Medal did anything for a writer, it would be to give his or her future books the benefit of the doubt, to give a chance to a book in which the author had taken a risk. I was also hurt by the chain store people's initial reaction, because I thought, *How many children have an alcoholic parent and know firsthand about parents who argue?* We talk so much about racial diversity in the children's book industry. But we're not talking at all about emotional diversity and class diversity, which are just as important.

When I was writing only YA fiction, I was just this guy operating from the sidelines, writing quiet urban stories like *We Were Here*. I was perfectly content, because I'd never had money in my life. Then the Newbery happened, and I found I had been placed in this new position. It made me think again about the stories I was putting into the world. It made it possible to take more risks. For instance, right now I am writing a picture book about a kid going to visit a parent in prison. That's not a very commercial idea. But I know that because I'm writing it, and Christian Robinson is going to illustrate it, it will get out there. In *Carmela Full of Wishes*, I wanted to explore a mixed-status family in which one person in the family is undocumented. Would this have been a commercial strategy when I was just this guy writing on the fringes? Books like these probably wouldn't even have gotten published. But now I can publish them, and that is what I want to put into the world.

ROBIE H. HARRIS

Born 1940, Buffalo, New York

As a graduate student enrolled at the Bank Street College of Education, in New York City, Robie H. Harris set out to become the kind of progressive teacher she had known and loved as a child growing up in Buffalo: a teacher who treated all young people with the utmost respect, paid close attention to the many ways that children change and grow from year to year, and understood that teaching is itself a process of continuous learning.

Bank Street has had a long tradition as an incubator for innovative teaching methods and as a proving ground for the creation of child-centered picture books, play materials, and educational media. It was as a student during the 1930s at Bank Street's Cooperative School for Student Teachers that Margaret Wise Brown, the author of *Goodnight Moon*, found her voice as a writer for children of the youngest ages. Twenty years later, a self-taught fledgling illustrator named Maurice Sendak spent time at Bank Street, too, strengthening his writing skills and sketching the nursery-school children for such picture books as *A Hole Is to Dig* and *A Very Special House*.

During Harris's Bank Street years, the school involved itself in the civil rights movement and in landmark efforts to improve the quality of children's television. Harris took part in both of these initiatives. Although she still had not decided to become a children's book author, more and more of her experiences were coaxing her in that direction, not least the admiration she felt for her cousin and close friend Elizabeth Levy, whose career in writing for children had begun to take off. In 1977, Harris got her feet wet as the coauthor with Levy of a nonfiction book called *Before You Were Three: How You Began to Walk, Talk, Explore, and Have Feelings*. Four years later, she took her first solo turn as the author of *I Hate Kisses* and began tentatively to think of herself as a writer. Then, in 1994, Harris's fifth children's book changed her life.

It's Perfectly Normal: Changing Bodies, Growing Up, Sex, and Sexual Health soon became widely known as a thoughtful, thoroughly researched young readers' guide to human sexuality—a topic that many parents felt uncomfortable discussing with their children. In print for more than twenty-five years, it has been translated into thirty languages and revised four times to reflect changing ideas about sexual identity and the way we talk about it. It also became one of the most frequently challenged books in recent history. In 2005, *It's Perfectly Normal* topped the

American Library Association's list of most frequently challenged books of the year and has made the Top Ten list many times since.

The heated response to the book—and to several of the more than twenty-five others by Harris that followed—thrust her into a highly visible public role as an advocate for freedom of expression as guaranteed in the First Amendment. When asked once why she continues to write books that stir up so much controversy, Harris replied, "How can we hold back writing about powerful feelings, or not include certain information children crave and have the right to know, simply because we are afraid?"

I had reviewed a number of Harris's books when we finally met several years ago at a writers' conference in Los Angeles. We recorded this interview at her apartment overlooking New York's Central Park and completed it with follow-up email exchanges.

———

LEONARD S. MARCUS: *What is the first book you remember caring about as a child?*

ROBIE H. HARRIS: It was *The Tall Book of Fairy Tales* [by Eleanor Graham Vance, illustrated by William Sharp]. I not only loved hearing my mother and my father read it to me, but I took that book to bed with me every night because I loved the stories it told. That book was my security blanket and lulled me to sleep for a number of months.

LSM: *Were other books important to you then?*

RHH: Yes, I had two sets of shelves in my bedroom: one with dolls in costume from around the world and the other with books. My parents and brother were readers, so books were a part of our everyday life at home.

This was in Buffalo, New York. Starting in kindergarten, I went to a progressive school where writing was emphasized. From kindergarten through eighth grade, the first fifteen minutes of every day were devoted to writing. Even in kindergarten, *every* morning each one of us dictated a story to our teachers, who wrote them down for us, and then we created the art for our stories— proof that I wrote my first book in kindergarten! I felt a sense of accomplishment when I finished making the cover for each book, and I pretended to read each book to myself despite the fact that I could not read yet.

LSM: *Once you could read, were you especially drawn to nonfiction?*

RHH: The *only* nonfiction book I can recall from that time in my life was *Book of Marvels*. We lived near Niagara Falls, which my family visited often. It was and is a marvel in every way. It was featured along with the Grand Canyon, the Acropolis, and other marvels around the world. This book brought the world to me. I became a nonfiction writer not because of what I read as a child but because I have always thought the best way to inform children is to tell them a good story. In my books for kids on sexual health, such as *It's Perfectly Normal*, I created two characters: Bird and Bee. Their voices represent the voices of kids. Their conversations show different possible reactions to the same facts and information in these books. In the Let's Talk About You and Me books for younger children, I tell the story through the conversations of two siblings, Nellie and Gus. These characters allow children to identify with the actual feelings kids have about the topics I am writing about. On classroom visits, young children have told me that when they "hear" Nellie and Gus, they have feelings such as "Oh, this is me! This is how I feel—or *don't* feel. Phew, my feelings are perfectly normal." My goal is to draw kids into the information in my books—information I believe will fascinate and interest them and hopefully help them make better decisions for themselves and their friends as they are growing up.

LSM: *Tell me more about your first school.*

RHH: I'm still in touch with a few of my classmates from that school. We talk about how we loved our time there because the teachers were so supportive of our ideas and always prompting us to think for ourselves by asking us questions. In fourth grade, we made volcanoes, which was fun because the goal was to make them explode. When mine didn't work on my first try, the teacher pressed me to figure out what had gone wrong. Soon, I was able to make my volcano explode just fine, and by then I understood why real volcanoes explode, too. It was a great way to study science.

A lot of the kids in my neighborhood went to the same school, so we would walk there together every morning and ride bikes together after school. We were a community—a community of learners who had free time together before and after school to play, to think, talk, agree, disagree, and argue. These are the same kinds of productive conversations that I still have with my friends and my editors, illustrators, and designers today.

LSM: *You must have passed through puberty together, too. How did the school handle that?*

RHH: Sex education was left to our parents. I grew up in a family in which science, information, and facts were thought of as fascinating and my right to have. My father was a radiologist, and whenever I visited his office, he would say, "Take a look at this." Once, he showed me a series of X-rays of a fetus so that I could see what a fetus looked like during its various stages of development. I was fascinated. My mother had studied biology, worked her way up in a lab at Children's Hospital in Buffalo, and would have become the lab's director had she not become pregnant—and been fired immediately. Because I had been given so much information about sexuality by my parents, I became an explainer to my friends.

In addition to telling me the facts about the science of sexual reproduction, my parents taught me that there was nothing about sex to be ashamed of. I don't know if they called it "amazing," but that was how they talked about sexuality. "Bodies can do this! Isn't that fascinating?" They also stressed that I had to know what was going on with my body so that I could stay healthy and safe.

LSM: *How old were you when your parents first talked about sexuality with you?*

RHH: I asked my mother about that once. She said she first talked to

me as soon as I asked the question "Where do babies come from?" I was four or five.

LSM: *How did you imagine your future then and in the years that followed?*

RHH: My mother and father always said my brother and I were to give back to people who were less fortunate than ourselves. My father often treated patients who were unable to pay him, and my mother did volunteer work in the community. To my parents, "giving back" meant that my brother was expected to become a doctor, which he did do, and I would become a teacher. I never questioned this. I edited my high school newspaper and college yearbook, and in college I majored in English literature. But I was not yet thinking of a career as a writer, let alone a writer for children.

My mother died suddenly in October of my senior year of college, a traumatic loss for me. This is probably why a lot of my picture books are about separation. After college, I moved to New York City. My first job was writing reports for the United Nations. I was going to apply to Teachers' College, Columbia University, when a friend told me that there was a progressive graduate school for teachers in Greenwich Village called Bank Street. I had never heard of it, but my friend said, "You've got to go to this place." I decided to see for myself and spent a whole day with one of the founders, Charlotte Winsor. At the end of that day, she said to me, "You're coming to Bank Street!" And I said, "Yes!" It was such a good fit, its view of learning so much like that of my school in Buffalo.

LSM: *What were your studies like there?*

RHH: The best course I took was Observing and Recording the Behaviors of Young Children. Each week we would observe a child for a two-hour stint and write down every movement, emotion, and word that child uttered. What was most powerful to me were the children's words. Today, observing and recording is still a powerful tool for my writing. Kids' words—and actions and emotions too—fuel the work I do and often find their way into my books.

Sometimes those words have resulted in one of my books being challenged or banned. For instance, many young children use the word "hate" or say "I hate you!" in conversation. And there are adults who believe that no child should ever say those words because they are "bad words," and saying them makes a child "bad," too. I remember times when my children were very young and got so angry that they said those very words to me. Each time, I felt like an arrow had pieced my heart. But then I would think, *They're not being bad. They're just angry with me. They love me, and they know I love them and will never leave them. So I'm not going to punish them, but I am going to talk with them about how their words made me feel so that they understand well that whatever they say has consequences.* I wrote about this in my picture book *The Day Leo Said I Hate You!* in which the young child in the story says "I hate you!" to his mother. On the next page, Leo wishes he could stuff the words "I hate you" right back in his mouth, but it was too late. This reflects the fact that emotionally healthy kids know when they have crossed a line and may, and often do, feel terrible about what they have just said. It's from experiences like these that children learn what they can and cannot say. Note that this is *not* censorship. It's learning to have respect and empathy for others and how to live in a civil society. Our society is becoming more and more uncivil these days, and I am very disturbed about that. But it's not because one child says "I hate you" to a parent or someone else. We need to help our children become civil. That's what growing up should be all about. I wrote about this again in my nonfiction picture book *Who We Are!*: "Saying mean things to a person, calling someone a bad name, or laughing at or teasing that person can make that person feel very sad or even very mad."

There have been informal complaints about this kind of thing in my books, which, while not formal challenges, can result in schools or parents deciding not to buy a book. Or this can result in a formal complaint that leads to a book being taken out of the library—banned.

LSM: *After you completed your graduate studies at Bank Street, did you begin teaching right away?*

RHH: Bank Street hired me as an assistant teacher. I was to work for a third of the year with sixth graders, a third with third graders, and a third with the four-year-olds. It was a wonderful way to start—or would have been but for the fact that three weeks into the school year, a newly hired teacher turned out to be an absolute disaster, and the school's director came to me and said, "You're the teacher now! You are taking over the six-sevens class," the equivalent of first grade. I was clueless about so many things and had to learn fast. But almost every day, one of the founders or senior faculty would observe my teaching, and at the end of the day we'd discuss what had gone well and think out loud together about a remedy for what hadn't. Over time, I became a better teacher.

After that very intense first experience, I returned to Buffalo for a year to teach at a public school. But I came back to Bank Street when their Head Start program, one of the first thirteen in the nation, was about to begin. I wanted to be a part of it, and I was put in charge of two programs: one for the parents, who were mostly teenagers; and the after-school program for the siblings of the Head Start kids. On the second afternoon with the kids, who were kindergartners through fourth graders, I said to them, "Let's go up on the roof."

This was something we routinely did with the Bank Street preschool kids as a way of introducing them to their neighborhood. Up on the roof, we could see the Hudson River, the Empire State Building, and more. Some even spotted the buildings they lived in. It was a view of New York City, their home, that they had never before had. When the kids pointed to the river, I said, "We can go down to the river. We can take a trip there." Their parents were caring but beyond overstressed: very low income, mostly single, and with little or no support. So it was not surprising that they had never taken their children on a trip like that. When I made this suggestion, the kids pushed back hard. They said, "We *can't* go down to the river." "Why not?" I asked. "Everybody who goes down there dies." "People push you into the river." "People get killed." "I can't swim. I'd drown." They had one fearful idea after another. I just listened, took notes, and thought, *I'm not going to take them down to the river—yet.*

LSM: *How did you respond to their fears?*

RHH: Around that time, I attended a lecture at Bank Street about photography and film that gave me an idea. What if I could give these kids cameras? Would that entice them to go out? Maybe the camera would act as a protective shield between them and a world they perceived as scary, and which in some ways really *was* scary. I thought that having cameras might make going out into their neighborhood fun and enable them to "see" that some of the things they feared weren't scary after all. I wrote a brief proposal and was funded to get Super 8 movie cameras for each kid, all the film we wanted, and the help of a wonderful filmmaker, Philip Courter. That's how I got the kids out on the street and eventually down to the river. I told them, "You can film *anything* that interests you." We would take walks around the neighborhood in whichever direction they chose. I did not impose any structure on them. They were free—uncensored. I named the film that came out of those walks *Child's Eye View*.

LSM: *Tell me more about the film and the experience of making it.*

RHH: At first, the children filmed themselves and their friends. Then they began to film things such as sides of beef hanging on a hook at a meat market, especially the blood dripping from the beef; a drunken man, whom one child identified as "my uncle"; a person asking for money, named as "a bum" by one child; an open manhole, which one child said people fall into all the time and die; the Hudson River, where several children agreed that people throw dead bodies or drown; a theater with a sign that said ADULT FILM, where one child said kids sneak in to look; some teenagers, whom the children called "bad bullies" and said were thieves; and a rat scurrying through some bags of garbage, which was labeled "adorable" by three of the children.

On later trips, they also noticed other, less fear-related things, like the produce and delivery trucks at a fruit and vegetable market; the big hole being dug at a construction site and the massive tunnels and wires that would bring electricity and water to that building; and the boats and ships on the Hudson River that were bringing bananas and other goods to their city. They began to ask lots of questions. Parents would come with us when the kids were filming, and in time the parents learned positive things about their neighborhood and began to talk with their kids about what they had learned during our walks. Seeing that happen was a joy.

LSM: *You also recorded the voices of the children talking about what they had seen.*

RHH: I felt that viewers of the film would want to hear the actual voices of the kids. After all, they were the best communicators of why they felt the way they did about their neighborhood, both before and after they had filmed it. As I mentioned earlier, recording the authentic voices of kids has always been a key part of my writing process.

LSM: *Soon after making* Child's Eye View, *you did some work for children's television.*

RHH: Yes—and I had my first real experience of censorship. After *Sesame Street* began airing in November of 1969, the *Captain Kangaroo* show, which was a long-running morning children's program on CBS, was feeling the competition and came to Bank Street for help. The producers asked us to create a weekly five-minute opening segment, including an original song, and I was one of three writers who was hired. The theme of our first segment was the rooms in your home. We turned in our work and were asked to come to CBS to visit the set and meet the Captain—whose real name was Bob Keeshan. When we arrived, the Captain said to us, "There's a little problem. You need to talk with our lawyers." So we took the elevator to the fifteenth floor, where the lawyers got right to the point. "We are going to have to cut the script. There's something in it that we absolutely cannot say on-air." The three of us were puzzled. "Oh, what is that?" we asked, trying to be gracious. "The word *toilet,*" said the lawyers. "It's a terrible word!" and they proceeded to give us a long, lawyerly explanation about why it couldn't be allowed in a segment about the rooms of a child's home. At this point, one of my colleagues, whose husband was a prominent attorney, spoke up. "Excuse me," she said. "I don't understand the problem, because we never talk about what goes in a toilet." The lawyers had nothing to say to this except "No, no, no. You are missing the point. It's a bad word!" Then I asked the lawyers, "Are you trying to censor what we wrote?" No one answered.

We lost that battle. We understood that CBS was worried about ratings—and worried with good reason about *Sesame Street*—and that they didn't want any negative publicity. But we were outraged because that sort of approach is not in the best interests of kids. Looking back, I think we should have made a public issue of it.

LSM: *You cowrote your first children's book,* Before You Were Three, *with your cousin, children's book author Elizabeth Levy.*

RHH: When my first child was born, I was amazed from the moment of his birth by how fascinating and interesting and in many ways competent and aware he was. My young nieces and nephews were amazed, too. They asked me lots of questions about the baby, which I realized was partly because they wanted to know what they had been like at that age, too. "How do you know he's hungry if he can't say so in words?" "Do you know when he is going to walk?" "How will he learn to walk?" Liz was with me a lot of the time. So we thought it would be interesting to write a book about kids' questions like these.

LSM: *A few books later came* It's Perfectly Normal. *Did you have the title right from the start?*

RHH: No, I had a very boring title at first, *The Facts of Life.* The title I finally chose came from my own children. At my kids' school, reproductive and sexual health were part of the science curriculum from the time they were four. One night at dinner, my fifth grader sort of whispered to my seventh grader, "Were there any questions about S-E-X today?" His older brother replied, "Oh, yes!" and started to laugh with a swagger, before adding knowingly, "And when your teachers talk about it, do they say, 'It's perfectly normal'?" "Yeah," my fifth grader replied, "and then we have a discussion, and sometimes the teachers will say, 'But *that* isn't normal. Or *that's* not healthy. Still, most things about sex are normal, although some are not.'" I knew then what my title needed to be. For me, *It's Perfectly Normal* has always been fundamentally a book about health, both physical health and emotional health.

LSM: *It is also among the most frequently challenged and banned books of all time. You must have known what you were getting into.*

RHH: Yes, I did know. But I didn't care that the topic was loaded or that the book might be banned. I felt that a book could be an effective way to get information to kids that most kids wanted and needed. However, at the time I decided to write it, well-meaning colleagues and friends, ten or twelve of them who agreed with me politically and about most other things, all said, "Don't write this book. It will ruin your career. You will never be published again." I was warned! The fear was that the organizers of book challenges and bannings, like conservative activist Phyllis Schlafly, would make me a target, and that publishers would be afraid to be associated with me. Of course, I was aware this material was loaded. That's why I knew that before I looked for a publisher for the book I would first have to find the perfect illustrator, so that together the artist and I could show publishers at the outset what we had in mind for illustrations.

LSM: *How did you meet Michael Emberley?*

RHH: I had known his father, Ed Emberley, for some time, and had gotten to know his family. At some point Michael had shown me his wonderful work. So, I already knew him by then.

LSM: *When you contacted Michael about your book idea, how did he respond?*

RHH: At first, I didn't tell him all that much about the project. But when he finally came right out and asked, "Okay, Robie, so what's the book *really* about?" I said, "It's a book about sex for kids." To which Michael replied, "I'll be right over!" We have had such a good time working closely together on *It's Perfectly Normal* and many other books over many years.

Michael saw the project as a challenge. I told him, "My mantra is 'If it's in the best interests of the child, it's going into the book.'" For instance, early on, there is a section titled "Making Love: Sexual Intercourse" and an illustration of a naked woman and man in bed together. When Michael showed me the drawing, I just said "Oh!" because I wasn't sure that it should be *that* direct. So he sat down, drew a quilt, cut it out, and covered the couple with it partway. We spent some time moving the quilt up and down, looking for the perfect place for it. It was like playing with paper dolls! Finally, I decided that Michael had been right all along, and that drawing has been in the book since day one. In *It's So Amazing!*, a book for younger children, there is a comparable illustration. Michael did add a blanket in that drawing.

LSM: *Let's talk more about your characters Bird and Bee. Bee sometimes does not want to know as much as Bird wants to tell.*

RHH: That was always my intention: Bird would be the kid who wants to know everything and can't stop asking questions. And Bee would be the more private, cautious one who thinks anything about sex and bodies is gross and disgusting but gets fascinated by the science. It's a rather stark dichotomy in the book. Bird and Bee, by the way, started out as two kids until I realized I didn't want to ascribe a particular body type or racial, ethnic, or gender identity to either of them.

When people ask me why any eight-year-old needs to know that there is an artificial hormone that can keep an egg and sperm from meeting each other and creating a baby, I think of Bird and say, "Maybe that's the fact that will amaze some child to the point of going on to become a biologist. So what is wrong with talking about it?" Kids find their own way to read the book. The child of a friend of mine insisted on reading it alone. A couple of hours later, her child declared, "Don't worry. I only read the parts about keeping bodies healthy!" The parent was quite sure that her child had read most of the book.

It had been suggested to me early on that I write two books: one for boys and one for girls. I said no to this suggestion because I wanted kids to learn to respect the bodies of any gender, so that they would not tease or shame others' bodies when they started to change in visible ways during puberty.

LSM: *Let's turn to the people who don't like your books. How do you hear about challenges or bannings? How does the news reach you?*

RHH: In various ways. Sometimes my publisher lets me know. Other times someone living in the community where a challenge has occurred contacts me. Or a librarian may call my publisher, or the National Coalition Against Censorship or PEN American Center may call with the news. Once my publisher and I know that a challenge or potential banning is under way, one or both of us contact NCAC and PEN, and together we decide the best approach. Most often, a letter that I helped my publisher draft is sent out to the librarian, bookseller, or teacher facing the challenge, offering our help and accompanied by a list of reviews and awards that make it clear why the book has value. Often, but not always, it is a joint letter from NCAC and PEN about freedom of expression and why a particular book needs to be available to kids.

LSM: *How does news like this make you feel?*

RHH: At first, I get a terrible feeling in the pit of my stomach. It's almost a physical reaction. And I think, *Why in the world did I ever write these books when a librarian or bookseller out there may have had threats, may have had to leave their job, may have been taunted in their community, may have had tires slashed?* And then I think of this one child. Do you want to hear a really upsetting story? Here's what happened.

On March 9, 1997, a journalist named Michael Sokolove wrote about *It's Perfectly Normal* in an article published in Philadelphia's

Inquirer Magazine. The article was titled "Sex and the Censors." As part of his research, he asked to accompany me on a school visit in New York City. I said that I couldn't give him permission to do that because a reporter's presence might make the kids feel less comfortable about sharing their ideas or asking questions. Instead I invited him to come to see me at my office and offered to arrange for him to talk with some of the experts with whom I consulted. To all of this he happily agreed. On the Thursday before publication of his article, I received an advance copy of the finished piece, and my heart sank when I came to the story of a court case involving child sexual abuse in which *It's Perfectly Normal* had played a part.

A ten-year-old girl in Wilmington, Delaware, had gone to the library with her mother, who told the girl that she could take out any book she wanted. She picked a copy of *It's Perfectly Normal*, which was out on open shelves. She took the book home and started to read it, turning straight to the chapter on sexual abuse. Then she went to her mother and, holding the book open to that section, said, "This is me." Her father was the abuser, and the girl had never talked to her mother about it before. In the trial that followed, the story of the girl and the book was told. After the father was convicted and given a sixty-two-year sentence, the judge commented, "There were heroes in this case. One was the child, and the other was the book." I later wrote the judge to say that I respectfully disagreed. Yes, there were heroes: the child, of course, but also her mother, who had established a strong enough bond of trust with her that her daughter could feel free finally to tell her what was happening. Another hero was the librarian, who had made *It's Perfectly Normal* so easy for a child to find. Because of these heroes, the abuse was at last stopped.

I have been called a pornographer, a child abuser—every name in the book, as the saying goes. But whenever I am called one of those names, I think of that ten-year-old girl. I wish we never had to talk with kids about any of these aberrant behaviors. But we have to do so because they already know about them to some extent and because kids have a right to have the accurate information that can keep them healthy and safe. They need to know how to get help to make any abusive behavior stop.

LSM: *The story about this girl shows why it does not work well to put a book labeled "controversial" on a restricted shelf, where it would be harder for a child to discover it.*

RHH: It doesn't work at all. I was once at an event for librarians where this question was discussed. One librarian reported that restricted shelving was her solution to dealing with controversial books. But another librarian got up to challenge that idea. She started by saying, "I know every family in my town. I see them all the time. I know their kids. I know their life stories. In my twenty years as a librarian, no kid has ever come up to me and said, 'By the way, I'm sprouting a few pubic hairs and I wonder if you could recommend a book for me?' So how can you keep these books on restricted shelves?"

LSM: *A parent has the right to decide what his or her own child, especially a young child, should read. How is the librarian or teacher's role different?*

RHH: I have had librarians say to me that they would never have my books in their own homes but they have them in their public library collections because in a democracy they see it as their job to offer the public a range of well-reviewed materials. I think that librarians like that are the real heroes.

I have also had superintendents of school systems—probably ten or twelve over the years—come up to me and say, "If you'd take out this or that section of your book, every child in my district would read it, and your sales would go up." I always say in response to their suggestions, "Thanks, but I can't do that. If I did, I would be keeping information from kids about sexual health that could help to keep them healthy."

I was attending a state library event when a librarian told me that my books had kept disappearing from the shelves in her library. She replaced them at first, but after a while, it was taking up too much of her small budget to do so. Then one day the books were all returned in a knapsack, with a note that read: "I took this book because I thought that no child or teenager should read it. Then my fourteen-year-old teenage niece got pregnant, and now I realize that children do need books like this."

But things don't always go so well. In Maine, a grandmother who had read about *It's Perfectly Normal* on a right-wing website was absolutely outraged. So she went to the Lewiston and Auburn, Maine, libraries and took all the copies of my book without checking them out. Then she sent each library a check in payment for the books. The librarians did the right thing. They sent back almost identical letters, thanking the woman for the checks, which, they explained, they were returning to her because they were libraries, not bookstores, and asking her to return the books she had taken. When the woman refused to cooperate, she was charged with theft, and a trial took place at which the woman went on and on for several sessions at taxpayer expense. This continued for so long that finally the judge simply ordered the woman to return the books and dropped the case. I thought that she should have been required to give service back to the city, although not at the library! In the meantime, the libraries from which the books had been stolen were flooded with new copies donated by people from all over the country who had heard about the case. There were so many copies that they were later distributed to other libraries all around the state of Maine.

LSM: *Did you attend the trial?*

RHH: No, because it would have just inflamed opponents of my book and not helped. When there is any kind of challenge, I stay away from that location while it is ongoing for that very reason. But I always offer to speak to the press, even though some reporters do not report accurately. And I often visit the library afterward.

Sometimes I have been lucky enough to meet the frontline defenders of my books. In 2002, at a hearing supposedly convened to discuss a bond issue, county commissioners in Montgomery County, Texas, ordered the immediate removal of copies of *It's Perfectly Normal* from public library shelves countywide. Present at the hearing was Jerilynn Adams Williams, director of the county's library system, who objected to the order, noting that a formal process existed by which anyone could challenge a book if they chose. The commissioners were not interested in following the formal procedure. Jeri, whom I came to know well, fought vigorously against the order for the next three months, at one point organizing a group called Main Street Montgomery, made up of local residents who thought that children should have access to *It's Perfectly Normal*. There was this big brouhaha in the press. The coverage was nonstop. Finally, Jeri went to the commissioners and said, "Aren't you getting tired of all this publicity? I told you at the beginning that we have a process at the library." She knew she had worn them down, and the commissioners agreed to withdraw their challenge and allow *It's Perfectly Normal* to remain in the young adult section of the county's public libraries.

Sometime after that, Jeri received an award from Planned Parenthood in Houston at an event that I also attended and that was picketed by anti-abortion activists. Jeri and I crossed the picket line together. People were yelling and screaming and giving out drawings of a boy having sexual relations with an animal, claiming that the drawing was from *It's Perfectly Normal*. It wasn't! Their claim was not true.

There have been other such urban legends about my books. Sometimes the truth is not told. Sometimes false stories are spread on the radio or the Internet. I always say, "It is your right to disagree with anything that I put in my books. But don't lie about what's in them, and don't pass on a lie. Who gets hurt? Those kids, those teachers, those health professionals, those families who might be kept from reading a book I have written and helped by that book that I have written." This to me is the bottom line on freedom of expression. As a reader, you have the right to speak out for or against whatever you read. As a writer, I have the right to write whatever I want to write—and I am just not going to stop.

SUSAN KUKLIN
Born 1941, Philadelphia, Pennsylvania

When her childhood dream of electrifying the world as a bal-
lerina did not go quite as planned, Susan Kuklin turned to other
challenging art forms to satisfy her creative longings. She studied acting, got serious about photography, and found rewarding work as a
photojournalist and book illustrator before becoming an author as well.
During a transitional period when Kuklin taught high school, she developed strong feelings of admiration for teenagers as a group and began
to think of them as both subject and audience for book-length word-
and-picture essays. She wanted to explore the special demands faced by
contemporary young people as they came of age in a fast-changing, often

inhospitable world. A family history of progressive political and social engagement made her choice of direction feel right.

As a photographer and author-interviewer, Kuklin has made it her mission to examine in depth subjects of urgent concern to young people that the media and society have glossed over or ignored. Her method is to build a series of narratives from extended interviews with a representative group of teens for whom a given subject has been a lived experience. Working within this framework, Kuklin has probed the realities of homelessness, the AIDS crisis, teen pregnancy, teen suicide, the American prison system, transgender identity, and the plight of young undocumented immigrants. While hardly light reading, books like *Beyond Magenta, Trial, We Are Here to Stay*, and *In Search of Safety* pack the dramatic punch of a fast-paced novel and pull readers so completely into their orbit that it is hard not to empathize with their young subjects' struggles or to come away from their stories without having learned something new about what it means to be human.

Librarians have consistently supported Kuklin's fearless forays into risky territory, signaling their approval by choosing her work for recommended books lists and making her titles available on open shelves. Perhaps the greatest surprise of our conversation was the news that the first wave of book challenges that Kuklin is aware of occurred so late in her career, following the release of *Beyond Magenta*, in 2014. Of course, she points out, there may well have been attempts to ban earlier titles, too, that simply went unreported.

Kuklin and I met not long after I reviewed her book *Fighting Back: What Some People Are Doing About AIDS* in 1989 for *Parenting* magazine, and we have crossed paths ever since at writers' conferences and friends' gatherings. It was a particular treat, and a challenge, to interview this impassioned, rigorous interviewer. We recorded our conversation on the roof deck of Kuklin's New York apartment.

LEONARD S. MARCUS: *How did you get interested in politics? Become an activist?*

SUSAN KUKLIN: My grandmother marched with suffragettes for women's rights. My mother marched for civil rights. I protested the war in Vietnam. Family dinners were filled with conversations about justice and history. My grandparents, who were immigrants from Russia and Ukraine, never let us forget that we were the lucky ones—lucky to be alive and lucky to thrive in a country whose ideals were based on a fair Constitution. Many members of my extended family disappeared during the Russian pogroms, in Nazi massacres and concentration camps, and, finally, in Stalin's gulag. As the "lucky ones," we had the responsibility, our grandparents said, to stand up and speak out for those less fortunate. *Do something!* That was the constant message at family gatherings. I listened.

LSM: *You grew up in Philadelphia, which is called the cradle of liberty because of its role in the American Revolution. Did that historical legacy mean a lot to you?*

SK: It does now. I love Philadelphia. But like most kids, I took my birth city for granted. Although we often visited Constitution Hall, the Liberty Bell, and Betsy Ross's house (my favorite; I don't know why), I always wanted to live in New York City. New York was like the Emerald City. I'd say to my parents, "New York is only ninety miles away! Why are we here?"

LSM: *And they said . . .*

SK: My father said, "In New York, there are just too many people. We would be little fish. In Philadelphia we are part of a community. We can be big fish. We can always take a train to New York and then come back to beautiful, peaceful Philadelphia." I didn't mind little fish.

LSM: *As a child, how did you imagine your future?*

SK: I yearned to do something creative. And I wanted to be where the action was. I wanted to know what was happening—the where and the when and the why—and I tried to figure out how I could get out into the world. First I wanted to be a ballet dancer. Like so many mid-century American girls, I took ballet class after school, and at age eight I announced to my parents that I was going to devote the rest of my life to dance. I told them that I was never going to get married, never going to have children, and that I needed to learn French because French was the language of classical ballet. My parents replied, "That's very nice, dear. Now eat your dinner!"

LSM: *You must have been a serious, determined child.*

SK: I thought I was normal.

LSM: *Were you an only child?*

SK: I was. But I was part of a large extended family who lived within a block of one another. We were always together.

LSM: *Did you have a mentor or other important influence on you as you were growing up?*

SK: I was fortunate to have some great role models. My grandmother for her love of literature and the arts. My grandfather for his kindness and sense of fairness. My mother and aunts for their passion for politics. My father for his fun—he was a great ballroom dancer. My uncle for his curiosity. I could go on . . .

I was the eldest of the grandchildren. My grandfather, who was a contractor, would take me to work with him. He called it "going on the job." One of my earliest memories is of sitting on a curb, lunch pails by our sides, eating with painters, carpenters, and plumbers. I also remember tagging along as Pop, as we called him, went to meetings with bank presidents and politicians. He treated everyone with whom he worked with the same respect, no matter the person's status. My grandfather's evenhandedness with people made a lasting impression.

LSM: *Many aspiring dancers bump up against insurmountable physical limitations. Did that happen to you?*

SK: Oh, yes. My physical limitation was evident early on. I couldn't do a split. I hate to admit this. The split was beyond my reach. Eventually I faced the hard truth that I was not made to be a ballerina. Even so, I continued to take dance classes for much of my life—I still attend dance programs—and I have authored or illustrated four dance books. It's such a pure art. An honest art. Dancers are some of the most delightful, dedicated people I know.

LSM: *What took the place of dance?*

SK: Theater. I majored in theater arts at New York University and also took acting classes at the Herbert Berghof Studio.

LSM: *I used to think that your books about dance were unrelated to your books about political issues such as LGBTQ rights and immigration. But they're all about freedom, aren't they?*

SK: For sure. For me, dance is the ultimate example of freedom of expression. Dancers and choreographers use their bodies to express an idea, a feeling, an opinion, a point of view. When you get right down to it, all my work is about freedom of expression.

LSM: *What was the high point of your acting career?*

SK: That was so long ago, it's hard to remember. I was a theater major throughout undergraduate and graduate school. Summers were spent working as an apprentice—two-dollars-a-day salary—in summer stock. I played Madge, the lead in *Picnic*, by William Inge, and I was a waitress on a TV soap opera. And though I enjoyed creating a role, getting into a character's skin, as it were, I much preferred directing. Directing a play is like painting on a huge canvas. So many creative elements—both visual and

intellectual—go into putting together a single play. I found directing very rewarding.

My problem was going to auditions. Auditions made me feel
like a piece of meat. I looked for any excuse not to go. To support
myself during this period, I took additional education courses so
that I could substitute-teach.

As a substitute teacher, I was sent to schools in Harlem and
on the Lower East Side of Manhattan. I loved teaching high school
students but not in a traditional way. One particular group of
students could not keep a teacher for an entire semester. They were
often truant. When they did come to school, they were rowdy and
paid no attention to the lesson. I was trying to teach Shakespeare,
and they were throwing things and laughing among themselves. It
drove me crazy that I couldn't reach them. One afternoon, out of
utter frustration, I stood in front of the door and said, "You're not
leaving until you tell me why you are not studying or doing any
of the work." After going around and around, all of us yelling and
screaming—me too—one boy blurted out, "Because we can't read."

Whoa! How's that for an honest answer! We decided to meet
secretly, before the official school day started, and study basic reading skills. The only person who knew about this was the school
custodian, who had the key to let us in. Every boy showed up.
Some of the parents came to class with breakfast for us. It was the
most beautiful experience of my life. Why go to some stupid audi-
tion when I could hang out with this fabulous group of kids who
were actually achieving something? I became a full-time teacher.

On Wednesdays, we would get dressed up and go on field trips to Broadway matinees. I knew a number of the Broadway stage managers, and they let the kids in for free. The kids began reading reviews in the *New York Times* to pick out which plays they wanted to see. Oh, how I loved those students. They are probably the reason I write for teens.

LSM: *Then you became a photojournalist. When did you get your first camera?*

SK: When I was in high school in Philadelphia, my uncle, who was a big influence on my life, bought a Leica. He taught me how to use the camera, and we went around town, taking photographs. Uncle Leonard taught me that the camera was a way to see life more intensely. Photography helped me appreciate that the world was a place of infinite possibilities—all one needed to do was look.

My first photograph was of an egg cooking in a frying pan. Very Man Ray. Then I began photographing friends. When I met Bailey, who became my husband, we talked about what we wanted to do with our lives. Bailey wanted a life in the academy, and I wanted to be a photographer. We married and moved to Knoxville, Tennessee, where he taught at the University of Tennessee law school and I became serious about being a professional photographer. (I must have really loved him to leave New York.) In preparation for our life together, Bailey spent his entire savings on a Leica camera for me. I studied the art of photography by scrutinizing the works of my favorite photographers, especially Walker Evans and Dorothea Lange. A local photography store in Knoxville let me use their darkroom. Photojournalism is not just about technique and looking at stuff. You need luck, and you need to be in the right place at the right time. I got lucky. I met two amazing women who were local volunteers for Planned Parenthood. They took me with them as they went deep into Appalachia to distribute health information to the women and families who were isolated from the outside world. The poverty and lack of resources there was astounding. Criminal. Nevertheless, the individuals I met were extraordinary. They were warm, gracious, and generous. I spent two years in the mountains, photographing families. I was learning my craft, for sure, but I was also learning about life. I put together a large photo-essay that eventually served as my portfolio when we returned to New York.

LSM: *How would you describe the subjects you are attracted to as a photographer and writer?*

SK: Hmm, I'm not sure how to answer this question. Photography is all about shapes—lines and circles—and color. That's what I look for when I'm actually shooting. But there's another part: I love the fact that the camera gives me access to meeting folks I would not otherwise meet. I love photographing people. I love faces. People are distinct, similar, and interesting—especially interesting.

LSM: *Tell me how you began making books.*

SK: When my husband and I returned to New York, I started making the rounds with my "Appalachian Families" portfolio. For the longest time I got no work, no work at all. There were just too many other photographers with great portfolios vying for the same jobs.

I had to come up with something to get an art director's attention. Instead of just presenting my portfolio, I came up with story ideas that I offered to write as well as photograph. So the magazine would get two for one: a photographer and a writer. Lo and behold, I began getting assignments. But my luck did not hold. Every magazine that hired me went out of business: *Look, Life, Cats*. My entire salary was made up of kill fees—partial payments made for work satisfactorily completed but not actually published. It was a mess. I thought I would never be a professional photographer. Then a good friend who was a professor at Columbia University received a grant to see if a chimpanzee could learn language. He needed a photographer to document the work, and he offered me the job. But first I had to learn sign language, the language used in the study, because chimpanzees do not have adequate vocal cords for speech. For the next several months, I signed with and photographed the chimpanzee known as Nim Chimpsky (named after the renowned linguist Noam Chomsky) as he learned language. Nim was living in a Columbia University–owned mansion in Riverdale along with a group of graduate-school caretakers! My photographs of Nim appeared in numerous magazines and in a children's book, *The Story of Nim: The Chimp Who Learned Language*, that came out of the project. That is how my career in children's books began.

LSM: *What came next?*

SK: I found more magazine work, most important, photographing the New York City Ballet as the great choreographer George

Balanchine created his last ballet. Magazine assignments were fun, glamorous even, but they were not fulfilling. The short deadlines were so stressful. I preferred spending long periods of time learning about and pursuing a project. Magazines don't allow you to work that way, but the children's book world does. So, that is how I finally found my professional home and my heart's desire—creating children's books.

The first book I wrote as well as photographed was *Mine for a Year*, the story of a thirteen-year-old foster child who was raising a puppy that would eventually become a guide dog. The young boy, George, was himself thought to be going blind. It was a powerful story. I proudly showed the first draft of the book to an editor friend. He barely got through the first paragraph before shouting, "BORING! Really, Susan, you can do better than this." I'll never forget those words. Embarrassed—devastated, actually—I went back to the drawing board. That's when I came up with the idea of writing in the first person. The rewritten version of the book met with my editor friend's approval, and I was off and running.

My second book was a picture book called *Thinking Big*, about an eight-year-old girl with dwarfism. The subject was one that other people seemed uncomfortable with, and I wanted to understand why.

LSM: *You interviewed Jaime, the eight-year-old girl, and her family. Did you enjoy that experience?*

SK: Every. Single. Minute. Jaime was the most wonderful child. She was joyous and self-confident. Her parents and brother were entirely supportive of her. What I learned was that Jaime was like any other eight-year-old girl, only she was little. That was the important lesson of the book. We remain friends.

LSM: *Since then, you have published more than thirty books for children and teens, including several on controversial subjects. How is it that* Beyond Magenta: Transgender Teens Speak Out *is the only book of yours that has been challenged, as far as you know?*

SK: I have no idea. Then again, authors don't always know when a book has been banned in a particular place. I believe that the American Library Association does not give out the names of the librarians whose book selections are being challenged unless the librarians themselves give permission.

LSM: *As someone whose work is about putting yourself in the shoes of others, can you empathize at any level with the people who challenge your books?*

SK: That's an interesting question. I suppose that I should empathize with my challengers. In all honesty, I do not. Although I strongly support a person's right NOT to read my books, I do not support those who try to impose their values on others.

LSM: *As you edited the interviews in* Beyond Magenta, *what were some of the hard choices you made?*

SK: Some might assume that interviewers simply plunk the interviewee's words on a page with no editing. Capturing a person on the page is a much more complicated process. It requires pulling together

pieces of interviews, adding observations and clarifications, and then choreographing the material into a coherent narrative. In addition, each chapter must provide new information. The decisions about what goes in and what stays out are based on the topic rather than simply on a person's biography. For example, one of the participants in *Beyond Magenta* told me about a number of sexual experiences that had nothing to do with being transgender. I left most of those comments out because it would have skewed the chapter. As always, I explained my decision to the interviewee for approval. I also had to decide whether or not to keep in all the f-bombs. I chose to retain some of them to be true to the voices of the people interviewed. To ensure accuracy and keep the material authentic, I always invite the participants to read finished drafts. In the end, I am responsible for every word that appears in my books.

LSM: *Why did you decide to make a book about transgender teens?*

SK: It started over a lunch between two colleagues. I wasn't part of the lunch. One person spoke of the need for more YA LGBTQ books—"you know, Susan Kuklin kind of books." To which the other replied, "Then why not ask Susan Kuklin to do one?" When the idea was presented to me, I thought it was an important topic, but it needed focus. At the time, I was working on a book about teenage inmates on death row, *No Choirboy*, but the LGBTQ theme kept living in my head. Meanwhile, there were news reports about transgender people being bullied, beaten, even murdered. I felt that young readers needed to know about this. I decided that my next book would focus on the "T" in LGBTQ.

LSM: *Do you hear often from your readers?*

SK: I hear from readers of *Beyond Magenta* more than those of any other book. I hear from kids who are isolated in small towns, who come from conservative families, who have been bullied. Their emails are filled with pain and longing. Their emails break my heart. Some kids write to say how important it was to see someone like themselves on the cover of a book. Four readers, three in the US and one in Japan, wrote to say the book kept them from suicide. It was worth writing the book for just those four kids.

LSM: *I thought it was interesting that the young people you interviewed had such different ideas about the extent to which they wished to be seen on the page.*

SK: Each chapter's photography was shaped to fit the individual's personality. After all, these portraits—text and photographs—were created so that the participants could take control of their own narrative. Nat, for example, who is a terrific artist and musician, agreed that their photographs should be classic, in the style of André Kertész, the great black-and-white street photographer. We privately titled their photo-essay "The Long Road with Musical Interludes." Cameron liked "blending stuff, having something girl and something boy and something neither." They came up to my studio with a suitcase filled with clothing, and we did a fashion shoot. Two fashion shoots. One person chose not to be photographed at all—too bad, because she is stunning. Another wanted his photograph in the book, but his family worried that it could be dangerous, so I photographed only parts of him—hands, torso, etc.

LSM: *The question of whether or not to show the teens you interviewed took on a whole new meaning in* We Are Here to Stay: Voices of Undocumented Young Adults. *Tell me what happened as you were working on that book.*

SK: The original photographs for *We Are Here to Stay* were in full color, except in one section, in the desert, which are in infrared and black-and-white. I am proud of those photographs, especially the portraits. Throughout the 2016 presidential election period, I worried about how the outcome of the election would affect the participants in the book. Everyone said not to worry, that the book would help move President Hillary Clinton's immigration reform forward. I worried. The book was designed and ready for print when the new president, who was not Hillary Clinton, was elected. The morning after the election, I called my editor, crying—hysterical, actually—and said that we can't publish the book. Long story short, we stopped the press and locked the layouts, edits, etc., in a drawer. I contacted the participants to let them know that everything was on hold, that we would do nothing to add to their stress, and that we would do nothing without their permission. It was a terrible time. Everyone was disappointed. But it was just too risky to leave these marvelous kids vulnerable to the whims of politicians. I assumed that the book would never be published.

After about a year and a half, with the contributors' involvement and approval, we all agreed that their experiences were too important to leave in a drawer. We decided to publish the book, but with changes to protect the participants.

We took out the photographs, leaving the caption and an

empty frame on the page. We used their first initial in place of their names, and we removed other identifiers. This was explained to the readers with the following statement: "Due to the uncertainty of the status of the DACA program at the time of publication, the photographs, names, and other identifiers of the participants in this book are being withheld." Someday I hope the book can be republished intact as it was originally intended.

LSM: *How do you choose your interview subjects?*

SK: In a way, my subjects choose me. The process of selecting people is a bit complicated because I will not say no to anyone who wants to participate. More often than not, I work with an organization, preferably a small grassroots organization. I talk with the professionals there and explain the object of the book and how I need to include as diverse a population as possible. Once the organization comes on board, the professionals there give me vague descriptions of their clients—no names—and I decide if their profile fits the topic. We balance the need to know about a person's background with the need for confidentiality. I look for diversity in their life experiences, ethnicities, and socio-economic positions. The professionals then tell their clients about me and give them my phone number. It is the client's choice whether or not to call.

LSM: *What about self-censorship? In conversations with your editors—or yourself—have you ever decided to leave out or otherwise change something that you thought might prompt a challenge?*

SK: Never. Challenges do not enter into the conversation. The only time my editors and I leave something out is when the material is not quite right for the book. For example, when working on *No Choirboy: Murder, Violence, and Teenagers on Death Row*, I interviewed a man who had been falsely accused of murder and put on death row even before his trial. He was a grandfather by the time he was exonerated and out of prison. I spent time with him in New York and in Alabama and wrote a long chapter about his experiences. My editor thought the focus of the book should be on the teens who were either on death row or serving a life sentence in a maximum-security penitentiary. I tried rewriting his story every which way because I wanted to tell his story. At one point, I interviewed his grandchildren and rewrote the chapter from their point of view. It did not work. Eventually I agreed to drop the chapter altogether. Is that censorship—or is it shaping a book? I believe it was shaping a book.

In another book, *Fighting Back: What Some People Are Doing About AIDS*, I interviewed a drug addict who had AIDS. He attempted suicide, was rushed to the hospital, and was revived. He recalled the moment of coming to and looking up at a bunch of smiling doctors. He'd shouted, "Oh, fuck!" My editor, Refna Wilkin, told me that I needed to take out the word *fuck* from the text. When I asked her why, she replied, "Let people challenge this book because they are homophobic. Let's not give them the excuse that they object to the book because of the language." I thought that was a powerful argument, and with the permission of my interviewee, I removed the quote. And yet this editorial decision continued to bother me. FYI, years later when the same editor and

I were working on another book, she casually said, "Oh, and by the way, Susan, you can keep all the *fuck*s in this one." Refna was a revolutionary editor for nonfiction books for young adults.

LSM: *Your book about AIDS was never challenged?*

SK: Not that I know of. I did have a few hostile interviews with print reporters and a phone interview on a right-wing talk radio show. The show's host said some pretty vile things about the people in *Fighting Back.* Even so, I was glad I went on air, because it gave me the chance to point out the host's hypocrisy and willingness to give his listeners false information. At one point, I told him, "You're doing a great disservice to your listeners, because you're not telling them the truth about this disease." Break for commercial. The end.

LSM: *Is it the library community that supports a book like that one?*

SK: Yes. Absolutely. Were it not for librarians, I would not have a career! They are not only the primary purchasers of books like *Fighting Back* and *Beyond Magenta*, but they are also the soldiers on the front lines who defend them, protect them, and put them into the hands of teen readers. I once met a librarian in Texas who said she kept a copy of *Fighting Back* under her desk and would whip it out for some of her kids and say, "I've got the perfect book for you." Too bad she had to hide it. Librarians know their children; they know their communities. Librarians are awesome.

LSM: *Why specifically was* Beyond Magenta *challenged?*

SK: In 2015, the book was placed on the ALA's list of ten most challenged books; it had been challenged because it dealt with homosexuality, incorporated foul language, was anti-religious, and was anti-family. I was particularly surprised by the last two complaints, about religion and family. *Beyond Magenta* is for and about family. The point of the book is to help families.

LSM: *It's funny and more than a little bizarre that the Bible appeared on the same Top Ten list on account of its "religious viewpoint."*

SK: The one affirming thing about being on the list was sharing it with the Bible.

LSM: *You show family members wrestling with issues that they don't always understand at first but about which they sometimes change their minds.*

SK: I have the privilege of spending time with the participants as they change and develop. While I was working on *Beyond Magenta*'s chapter called "Every Girl Is Different," Christina's mother said, "I have a few things I want to say about this. Tell Susan I want to be in the book." Although I thought I should keep the focus on teens, I am glad that we included one mom so that parents could see her process of evolution. It didn't happen overnight. At first Christina's mom was unsupportive when her middle son told her that he was gay, and livid when her youngest son told her he was transgender. In time, she became a fierce defender of her children. I'm so impressed with Christina's mom. And she's proof that the book is pro-family.

    In addition to the formal challenges, a few, not many, people in the trans community questioned a cis person writing a book from the point of view of transgender participants. I understand and appreciate the distinction. My objective is from a different point of view. We all have stories. We don't all have the microphone to tell our stories. I have a mic. The participants in my books define themselves in their own terms.

LSM: *What do you think about the larger question of who has the right to tell whose stories?*

SK: That's a powerful and important question. In my view, writers write what's in their heart. I write about various people and their cultures because I believe, I strongly believe, that we need to know one another. We need to read one another. This is something I've cared about my entire life. I hope that my books are honest and respectful and that they open doors for other writers, because I feel tremendous respect for the people who bravely come forward to reveal who they are. Another writer who is part of a particular group will approach a subject differently. And that's great. There's plenty of room at the table.

DAVID LEVITHAN
Born 1972, Short Hills, New Jersey

Must a writer have "suffered" to produce lasting, meaningful work? Maybe not, to judge by David Levithan's steady, easygoing, buoyant example. Levithan has said, "I won the parent lottery. . . . And then I went and won the friend lottery." Life as a young gay man growing up with solid emotional support from the people closest to him became a theme of his first novel, *Boy Meets Boy* (2003), which helped move LGBTQ fiction beyond the confines of teen "problem fiction." Levithan cast the story as a romantic comedy set in a largely tolerant small-town community that one reviewer aptly dubbed Gaytopia. The title of that debut novel was certainly an attention-getter, and *Boy Meets Boy* proved to be a wildly popular and influential book. Partly for that reason, it triggered a flurry of challenges at school libraries.

Within ten years of its publication, as the struggle for LGBTQ rights registered significant gains, *Boy Meets Boy* lost much of its initial shock value and came to be regarded as mainstream YA literature. Levithan, meanwhile, continued through successive novels to open new territory in the rapidly expanding discussion about gender and identity and to experiment as a writer. In *Two Boys Kissing*—another book with an unapologetically up-front title and close-up cover photo to match—he intensified the narrative by incorporating an elegiac, Whitmanesque element of collective memory: chorus-like voices of the dead speaking for the generation that had borne the brunt of the AIDS crisis, offering later generations their encouragement and a sobering sense of historical perspective. In a lighter key, he framed *Hold Me Closer* as the script for an over-the-top musical about Tiny Cooper, the "world's largest person who is also really, really gay."

An outgoing person who has always put friendship high on his list of life's priorities, Levithan has written novels collaboratively with John Green, Rachel Cohn, David Ozanich, and Chris Van Etten and has also worked closely with fellow writers from the publisher's side of the desk. At nineteen, Levithan received an internship at Scholastic, and he has remained at the company ever since, in recent years as Scholastic's editorial director and the founder of the PUSH imprint, dedicated to discovering new talent. "These are exciting times in YA publishing," Levithan told England's *Independent* as *Hold Me Closer* was about to be released. "We're looking for diversity, and also diversity within that diversity."

I first heard Levithan speak publicly about the issues surrounding book banking in November 2017 at a National Coalition Against Censorship event honoring him as a defender of free speech. We created this interview through an exchange of emails.

———

LEONARD S. MARCUS: *How would you describe yourself as a child?*

DAVID LEVITHAN: I am sitting across the kitchen table from my mom right now, and you have no idea how tempting it is for me to pass the laptop over to her to answer this question. But since it's "describe yourself," I'd say I was happy, rambunctious, curious, and a bit of an overachiever (at least when it came to memorizing state capitals).

LSM: *When people asked you what you wanted to be when you grew up, what did you say?*

DL: I recall being all over the place as far as my aspirations. Read me a book about a fire engine, and I'd want to be a firefighter. Read me a book about a president, and I'd want to be president. The closest I can come to truly answering this question, in terms of the thought I gave to it at the time, would be to say, I did not want to be Luke Skywalker. Han Solo or Princess Leia, yes. Chewbacca in a pinch. But not Luke.

LSM: *Were you a very verbal child? A big reader? What were the first books that meant a lot to you?*

DL: I am still convinced that everything you need to know about me and my childhood is that I was profoundly, unalterably devoted to *Alexander and the Terrible, Horrible, No Good, Very Bad Day.*

Which is to say, my sense of injustice was loud, and perhaps a little too self-centered. And that I was a young Jewish boy in the suburbs with understanding parents. Also, I cared about my sneakers and found the notion of Australia attractive.

LSM: *When did writing become an important outlet for you?*

DL: By third grade I was writing stories and focusing on word choice; by fourth grade, I was putting together my own underground newspaper; by fifth grade, I'd written a play for my class (about . . . a fifth-grade class, of course). So I think it's safe to say that my elementary school teachers—well, most of them—were encouraging. And I took that encouragement and ran with it.

LSM: *Your character Paul in* Boy Meets Boy *says, "I've always known I was gay, but it wasn't confirmed until I was in kindergarten." Is Paul in that moment also speaking for you as a young child?*

DL: Funnily enough, my kindergarten teacher *did* bring up to my parents that I was playing too much with the girls and might be gay. (This was in the 1970s. I like to think that nowadays she'd say I was defying gender norms and leave it at that.) Alas, my kindergarten teacher's speculations were far ahead of my own self-awareness. Were I growing up now, I have no doubt I would be one of the kids who comes out at twelve. But the 1980s didn't do as good a job of clueing me in from the start.

LSM: *Did you have a mentor or role model who had a special influence on you early on?*

DL: On every level, I am who I am because of my parents. I had lots of great teachers and amazing friends, but when it comes to worldview, it's all my parents. And I don't think the writing I do can be separated from my worldview. In *Nick and Norah's Infinite Playlist*, I talk a lot about *tikkun olam*, the Jewish belief that the world is broken and it's our job to piece it back together. My parents engaged in the world to try to piece it back together and taught me to want to do that. So my characters often aim to do that, too.

LSM: *How did your professional life get started and evolve?*

DL: Long story short, I lucked my way into an internship at Scholastic in the summer between my sophomore and junior years of college. One of my jobs there was to assist Bethany Buck, the editor of the Baby-Sitters Club series. I found that putting myself into the head of a group of thirteen-year-old girls was remarkably easy (and remarkably fun) . . . and I've been at Scholastic ever since. I started with a focus on middle-grade paperback series, then was able to start a YA imprint, PUSH, for new writers. Since then, I've worked on everything from the Baby-Sitters Club to the Hunger Games books.

LSM: *When you began working in publishing, what kinds of stories were being told about the life of gay teens? What stories were not being told that you thought needed telling?*

DL: With some notable exceptions, gay teen characters were secondary and/or defined by shame and misery as we hit the mid-nineties. We were still in the "problem novel" stage, where being queer was approached as a problem, not an identity. And the problem was more often than not the queer character's, not the problem of the people who were around them. Again, there were some authors (shout-out to Nancy Garden and Francesca Lia Block) who were trying to disrupt this narrative . . . but the misery/shame/problem narrative kept repeating over and over.

LSM: *How has being an editor changed you as a writer, and how has your writing changed you as an editor?*

DL: I understand both sides of the equation better now, and I understand the bigger picture better now. Certainly one of the benefits of being an author is that we get all the direct feedback from readers—all the midnight-written thanks and the people coming up to say, "Your work changed my life." As an editor you certainly have the same impact, but it's less direct.

LSM: *You have spoken about Francesca Lia Block's Weetzie Bat books as an inspiration to you. What specifically about the books moved and encouraged you? What do you love about them? I recall feeling that she was writing in her own language in a way that only a few writers can.*

DL: I could probably write a dissertation on everything I learned from Francesca Lia Block's books. *Boy Meets Boy* would not exist without *Weetzie Bat* coming before it, and none of my other books would exist if *Boy Meets Boy* hadn't started it off.

The most important things about Block's books, to me, were their embracing of queerness (of all kinds), the musicality of their language, and their acknowledgment of the radical power of knowing who you are and knowing your own joy. What she could achieve with the characters of Duck and Dirk in the first Weetzie Bat book still astonishes me. They can't be on the scene for more than twenty pages total, and yet they made me smile and made me sob and, most of all, showed me that their love was more powerful than hate or shame or even the threat of death. They were both wildly outlandish and deeply human at the same time. Was this in part because I was mapping myself onto them as I read the book? Of course. But I'd never been given such a landscape to map myself onto before. And that was eye-opening and heart-opening, and it galvanized the way I saw what stories could do.

LSM: *The legendary editor Margaret McElderry once said, "There is always a fine line between censorship and editorial judgment." What do you think of this statement, and how would you draw the line between the two?*

DL: I'm going to respectfully disagree. I think there's quite a chasm between censorship and editorial judgment. First off, editors offer suggestions and guidance; they don't dictate or prohibit this or that. Also, whenever I edit, I am engaging with the story on the story's terms, not through the lens of what potential censors might say. I don't let them into the room when I'm writing. Why would I let them into the room when I'm editing?

LSM: *What prompted you to write* Boy Meets Boy?
DL: It started as a short story that was spurred on by a conversation

with a friend of my best friend. He had grown up in a religious family in a conservative town and hadn't been able to be himself until he escaped. Hearing his story, I wanted to rewrite it—just like I wanted to rewrite the ending of Patty Griffin's song "Tony," which is about a gay kid's suicide. And I decided to rewrite it by getting as far away from the "problem novel" as I could get, instead using romantic comedy as my base.

I genuinely didn't realize I was writing a novel at first. (Had I said to myself from the start, *I'm going to write a dippy, happy gay YA novel*, I would probably have been too intimidated to plunge in.) But slowly the short story got longer and longer, and I realized I was writing the gay YA novel I'd been hoping to find as an editor, to break that shame narrative, and to better reflect the happy gay life that my friends and I were living.

The awesome part, of course, is that while I was in my own apartment, writing the novel, there were a number of other authors who had a similar impulse—Brent Hartinger, Julie Anne Peters, Maureen Johnson, Lauren Myracle, and Alex Sanchez, to name a few. And 2003 ended up being the year that turned the tide for queer YA.

LSM: *Second novels are said to be the hardest to write. Was that true for* The Realm of Possibility?

DL: I always tell my writers to try to finish their second novels before their first one comes out—and I did that, so I wasn't intimidated by the reaction *Boy Meets Boy* ended up getting. I also decided to try a different form—a verse novel told from twenty different points of

view—so my second novel wouldn't be a carbon copy of the first. That helped.

LSM: *How did you first learn that* Boy Meets Boy *had been challenged?*

DL: I heard much more about preemptive censorship—that's when libraries and schools refuse to purchase a book for their collections—rather than outright challenges for *Boy Meets Boy*. I knew this was a risk of the title; you could judge it without having to read it! But it was more important to me to have a book that kids could see on the shelf and know exactly what it was.

If you look at the list of book challenges from the 2000s, you will see that Brent Hartinger's *Geography Club* (about a gay-friendly school club hiding itself as a geography club) appears much more frequently than *Boy Meets Boy* and *Rainbow Boys*. Why? Because, whereas with *Boy Meets Boy* and *Rainbow Boys* you could see the title and say, "Ah, I will keep that gay book from my shelves," you actually had to read *Geography Club* to know what it was about. So it got on more shelves in communities that would then try to pull it when they found out what sat between the covers. Both kinds of censorship are wrong—one is just more visible to the public.

The resistance to *Boy Meets Boy* was most noticeable in situations where I was directly involved—whether during the Kalamazoo protests against the book, which I will get to in a moment, or when I was disinvited from a school visit on my way to the school, or when people would leave vitriolic "reviews" on Amazon that didn't have anything to do with the book and had everything to do with the "sinfulness" of my identity. Some of this was censorship, and some of it was homophobic attack. But I had plenty of allies to help me fight the good fight and show gay teens that they deserved representation in our literature as much as anyone else.

In 2005, the Kalamazoo Public Library invited me to do a reading, combined with a program for local gay teens and adults to tell their stories. At some point during the day, we learned that a group calling itself Students for America was planning to picket the library. (One of the "students" said that my book encouraged gay sex among kindergartners, which was, to put it mildly, a misreading.) The library and the local community heard this was going on, and when it came time to open the doors, with camera crews from all the local newscasts outside, there were about fifteen protesters and three hundred audience members defying them.

Whenever my books have been challenged, the brilliant apparatus that fights censorship within the YA community has kicked in. Random House Children's Books has been engaged, the ALA has been engaged, the NCAC has been engaged. After a while, I realized the one person who didn't have to be engaged was me—these defenders were there to protect free speech, and the burden of defense didn't have to fall on my shoulders.

LSM: *How has the experience of having your work challenged affected you personally?*

DL: I am lucky, because I am incredibly well versed in how important and meaningful YA novels are. Long before I wrote my own books, I could see the positive impact that the books I edited could have on readers. Even when someone is being hostile, I can contextualize it into the greater good we do. And, let's be honest: it's never the teens who are hostile. Never. And I have pretty thick skin when it comes to angry adults, especially if it's clear that they haven't read the book they're criticizing.

That said, the fact that my book *and* my identity are being attacked at the same time isn't particularly pleasant. And if you want to rub me the wrong way, say that evergreen phrase: "You must be so happy that your book is being challenged—you'll sell so many more books!" The response to which is: "Yes, more people in that community are likely to read my book now. But it also means that the queer kids and allies in that community have to defend themselves and the book in the place where they live, and it means that there are likely librarians or teachers who have put themselves in the line of fire in order to defend the book." Intellectually I know free speech will prevail—it almost always does—and I know that some good conversations will come out of it. But it's still harrowing to have to face such intolerance on your home ground, and it never feels good to know that people have to go through that.

LSM: *Did you think of the title—and cover design—of* Two Boys Kissing *as an act of defiance?*

DL: As with *Boy Meets Boy*, I wanted the title and the cover to reflect what was inside the book. I knew the cover was groundbreaking, but I also knew that it was pretty pathetic that it had taken so long to break that particular ground. Nobody—no publisher, no bookseller—blinked at all, or hesitated at all, with the cover . . . which I think showed that I wasn't the only one who was ready for it.

LSM: *As a creator of novels with characters who are not just caricatures, can you imagine your way into the minds of the people who have challenged your books? How do you understand their motivations and actions?*

DL: Sure. We're all human. In this particular case, they just happen to be wrong. Their convictions may come from a genuine place (usually born out of a genuine fear) . . . but they're still wrong.

LSM: *What have you learned about the role of libraries in our country?*

DL: I've learned that most librarians are fierce defenders of intellectual freedom. And those who aren't—well, sometimes their views change over time, and sometimes we just have to wait for a younger generation of librarians to take their place.

LSM: *Would you agree that library book awards play a role in countering attempts at censorship?*

DL: I think any praise or award helps, in that they give a shorthand answer to the rather subjective question of literary merit, which is often a book's first method of defense.

LSM: *How have your books fared outside the US?*

DL: There was a lot of controversy about the release of *Boy Meets Boy* in the UK, particularly in Scotland, because it happened to coincide with the repeal of a law that prevented homosexuality from being mentioned in schools. But, as in the US, even with controversy, the book has had a long, good life there.

LSM: Two Boys Kissing *ranked number eleven on the ALA's 2019 list of most frequently challenged books, and the majority of listed titles were books with LGBTQ themes. How would you assess the extent to which openness to such books has changed compared with when you wrote* Boy Meets Boy?

DL: Yes, I was number eleven on the Top Ten—quite a distinction! But in truth, *Two Boys Kissing* made the list for 2018 as part of a group of LGBTQIA+ books that a man in Iowa decided to burn in front of a library. And while all of the books' defenders were successful, and they replaced the books he burned many, many times over, he still got on the national news for what he did. So, in a way, he got what he wanted. And people who want to attack LGBTQIA+ rights will always see the attack of books as a shortcut to getting the attention that they want. So they keep doing it, even though they nearly always fail in preventing the books from getting into the hands that need them.

LSM: *You have said that a great many of your readers write to you. Would you share the gist of a few messages that have meant a lot to you?*

DL: When I started, I got a great many emails from teens who'd never seen themselves in a book before. I don't get as many of those emails anymore . . . because there are so many books out there for them, and more good ones each week. And some of those new books are written by people who saw themselves in *Boy Meets Boy* over a decade ago. I couldn't be happier about that.

MEG MEDINA
Born 1963, Alexandria, Virginia

Looking back at her years as a Virginia high school teacher through the lens of her far more public current life as an acclaimed author and recurring target of book challengers, Meg Medina says, "I feel like I created a classroom that was exciting for my students. But I think if I were teaching today I would probably be fired, because I often picked a wide variety of books and short stories to share with my students that weren't on any approved curriculum."

Medina spent her earliest years in a working-class, Cuban American household in Queens, New York, where the oral tradition was alive and well. Her *abuela*'s vivid stories of Cuban life deepened Medina's connection to her family heritage and helped anchor her in a social environment that was often quite hostile to Latina girls. Her discovery of books and the written word—both in English and Spanish—became another vital lifeline that pointed her toward college, a teaching career, and eventually the rigorously honest and culturally nuanced fiction writing for young readers that she has made her vocation.

As a novelist, Medina has been unflinching in her examination of the emotional and moral hurdles that young people, especially Latina girls and teens, face when, on top of navigating the usual challenges of growing up, they must also make their way as members of a minority culture, in many cases from an economically disadvantaged position. Often taking her own experiences as a point of departure, she has amplified and transformed autobiographical material into culturally astute, proudly feminist narratives with a universal human dimension. "Going from girlhood to womanhood is a crazy, hard, fantastic journey of figuring out what the engine of your power is," she once told an interviewer, "and that's the story I want to keep offering girls."

Medina has received many of the most prestigious awards in her field, including the 2012 Ezra Jack Keats New Writer Award for *Tía Isa Wants a Car*, the 2014 Pura Belpré Award for *Yaqui Delgado Wants to Kick Your Ass*, and the 2019 Newbery Medal for *Merci Suárez Changes Gears*. She has made pointed good use of the public platform that has come with this recognition. As a long-serving member of the advisory committee of the nonprofit advocacy organization We Need Diverse Books, Medina has championed efforts to press for a more fully inclusive literature for young people and a publishing industry to match.

We first met over lunch in 2018 at the summer residency program in writing for children at Hamline University, in Saint Paul, Minnesota, and found that we had a lot to talk about. Medina was home, in Richmond, Virginia, when we recorded this conversation by phone.

———

LEONARD S. MARCUS: *Tell me about your childhood memories of story-telling at home.*

MEG MEDINA: In my family, storytelling had to do with trauma and with whatever was happening to us. My family had arrived from Cuba, and when I was growing up in Queens, my babysitter was my grandmother. Because she had only an eighth-grade education, my grandmother couldn't help me with my homework, so when I came home from school, our activities consisted of watching Spanish-language television together and her telling me stories— fabulous, wildly inappropriate stories about her life in Cuba. She had such good timing! She would pause at the exciting part, bringing me right to the edge of my seat. "You won't imagine this!" she would say.

Her stories were entertaining, and they gave her a chance to remember her life in Cuba: her town, her friends, her family, a way of life that she had understood. Telling stories was also her way of attaching me to what had come before me, and of showing me that I belonged not only to this sparse and difficult existence we had in Queens but also to something else: a community of people who loved me and who had done interesting things in the past. My grandmother's stories made me want to reach back to my Cuban family, and they made me curious about what my life might have been like if I had been raised in Cuba. They opened my mind to new ways of thinking about myself, including as a storyteller. My grandmother gave me an ear for it.

LSM: *You grew up bilingual. Where were the lines drawn for you between Spanish and English?*

MM: My mother spoke English, but not terribly well, and in our home she spoke only in Spanish to my sister and me. It was a deliberate decision on her part. She wanted us to know Spanish as well as English. This was in contrast to many immigrant parents of earlier years who would say to their children, "No, speak only English." I learned English from the TV show *Romper Room*, from the children I played with outdoors, and at kindergarten. I picked it up fairly quickly. My uncle taught me how to read in Spanish. When he arrived from Cuba via Spain, he ordered some Spanish-language books from a store in Miami, sat me down, and helped me practice, starting with a rhyme that translates: "A-E-I-O-U / A mule knows more than you!" It was glorious. I remember feeling so excited to be able to unlock Spanish and follow a story on the page. I'm fascinated by biculturalism and the places where English and Spanish intersect. That's what I'm mining: the interplay of the two languages and cultures.

LSM: *Did you study Spanish in school?*

MM: Yes, in seventh and eighth grade. Then in high school I was allowed to take independent-study Spanish, and I read Federico García Lorca and all kinds of other great writers.

LSM: *Your young heroines are very outspoken. Were you like them as a girl?*

MM: Not as outspoken as Merci! I wish I had been. Pieces of me are in all of my characters, but I've also given each one of them characteristics that I didn't have. I want to write fiction, not memoir: to fictionalize and have control over my characters in a way that I did not have control over the people in my life.

LSM: *Merci speaks about "the crossing guard in her head" as she learns to edit herself in social situations, especially those involving anger.*

MM: That's a skill I am still working on! In *Yaqui Delgado* and *Burn Baby Burn*, both girls have private realities that they do their best to keep secret. They're engaged in a kind of self-censorship as they look for the easiest way to survive. Both find out, eventually, that there is no hiding from yourself. It can be enormously risky and potentially painful to allow certain aspects of your personal life to come out into the light, but there is also a cost to keeping them secret. That's what Nora López and Piddy Sanchez both have to learn.

LSM: *What role does memory play in your work?*

MM: It's the engine, really. I begin so often with memory. I will sit and think back to myself at a particular age. I will remember a question I couldn't ask or a problem I could not solve and ask myself why. What was I afraid of? First loves. Deaths in the family. Longings. Fears. Particularly brutal arguments. The feeling of being at the mercy of the world, and how that looks when you're eight versus when you're twelve or seventeen. Then also the collective memories of Cuba, my family, and who they were. It becomes a portal for me. I cook those memories, and cook them and cook them, and change everything, until I have a new book.

LSM: *Has your approach to fiction writing changed?*

MM: Early on, I wanted to capture magical realism and the sound of Spanish for English-dominant Latino kids. I was writing in English but with that flavor. That in itself felt magical to me, and it sounded most like the voice of my grandmother in my head. But a more contemporary voice has allowed a more direct mining of my experience. When I write in that voice, I'm more in the mind of the character and of the story she's trying to tell me.

LSM: Yaqui Delgado Wants to Kick Your Ass *seems to mark the start of that change.*

MM: I don't feel that I made the decision alone. I had been invited by the writer Marisa Montes to contribute a short story for an anthology of stories about young Latinas at a turning point in their lives. It was such an honor to be asked. At first I had no idea what to write. Then I realized that one of the biggest turning points for me was when I got bullied in the seventh grade and every light inside me just turned off. I became very cut off from my family, very bitter, very suspicious. It was a broken feeling that lasted for years. I hadn't been like that as a kid. I had been really open and connected. Despite problems economic and otherwise, I had generally been a happy kid. So I thought, *What would this look like as a story?* I pretended at first that nobody was going to see it.

Then Marisa passed away, and the anthology never came to be. When my editor read the story, she said that she really liked my character Piddy, and if I could expand the story into a novel, she would buy it. That became the assignment. I expanded it to be about all the things I wondered about at that age: my relationship to my parents; my sense of my own body and what it was to be a girl; what it was to be a Latina—all of those things. Everyone sees *Yaqui Delgado Wants to Kick Your Ass* as a book about bullying, but Latina girls also understand it as a book about identity. That's what they want to talk about with me.

LSM: Yaqui *has been frequently challenged, in part because of its title. What considerations went into that choice?*

MM: The title came from Kate, my editor. It was always the opening line of the book, in which the entire first chapter is very close to a scene from my own life in the seventh grade at Junior High School 189 in Queens. It seemed fair to me for that line to appear inside the book, and it didn't seem particularly racy considering that it is a YA novel. *Ass* is a word that I am very confident high school students know and use.

But Kate's suggestion to have it be the title was a different matter. I thought she was crazy, and at first I said no. I had practical concerns having to do with how the book would be introduced in public—at school assemblies, for example, where there are always constraints on what language is allowed and what isn't. Another concern was, did I want to be perceived as someone who is coarse? For a Latina writer, that is an issue, a *thing*: not to be perceived as a vulgar person who uses "bad" language. It took a while for Kate to prevail, but she is fearless, and she did so by asking me whom I had written the book for. The truth is that I didn't write it for the librarians or the teachers or principals or the mothers. I wrote it for the girls who are in the crosshairs of a bully. When I thought of it that way, I realized the title would speak strongly to them. Kids who are being bullied are carrying a secret, a secret sense of shame. They're living in a kind of no-man's-land. So it seemed to me that the title would give them permission to pick up the book and see what's inside.

Another consideration was that my mother was alive at the time the book title was being decided. She had always been very buttoned-up and very conscious as an immigrant woman of not calling ugly attention to herself in any way. I was concerned about what she would think. I told her the title at dinner one night and said, "Mommy. Mami, *mira*, do you remember that girl who bullied me in junior high school?" She did remember. We talked a little about that, and then she said that, although she didn't like the title of my book, she could remember her own bully from school. This was something she had never spoken about before, and it sparked a good conversation. It was a nice moment for us.

I had lots of moments about books with my mom, especially late in her life. My mother and I had had a somewhat difficult relationship. She was very consumed with practical issues, like having enough money, and she had wanted me to have a secure job with benefits rather than to be a writer. I think she was often depressed. Growing up, I was much closer to my aunts. But when my mother became ill with cancer in her mid-eighties, I brought her and my Tía Isa to live with me. It became a time for us to get to know one another as women and to finally make peace. Books had always managed to find their way into my life, and at the end of my mother's life, books found a way to create a closed circle for us.

LSM: Yaqui *was well reviewed, but then the challenges began.*

MM: The first sign of trouble came when a schoolteacher in Cumberland, Virginia, a town not far from where I live, reached out to me about an anti-bullying assembly she was planning for fifth to eighth graders. *A perfect matchup to my book*, I thought. But in the days leading up to the event, the teacher emailed me to say that her principal had just seen the title of my book and was concerned about it. I could still speak to the students, she said apologetically, but I was not to mention the title of my book or show a slide of it, or use "coarse language" when I gave my presentation. Aside from the insult of asking an author to agree to such an arrangement, I felt also a complete lack of any understanding of what children who are being bullied are actually going through. The school's request that I distance myself from the language of bullying—language that I had intentionally embraced—struck me as an insult to the students they were trying to serve in an anti-bullying assembly.

I wrote back a long email, explaining why these conditions were unacceptable and suggesting that concerned parents be given the chance to have their children opt out of the assembly. As I wrote in a blog post soon afterward: "*No dice. The ax fell yesterday* when the principal emailed me to say that our visit was canceled. He explained that although he'd once been an English teacher, he had 'other considerations' as a school principal. *Wow, I wanted to ask. What happened? And what could those considerations be, exactly?*"

The event had been scheduled for Banned Books Week, and when the school superintendent was interviewed by the press about what had happened, he responded by saying that my book did not reflect Cumberland's "community values." He may even have made a coded reference to it being more of an "urban" book. It was just appalling.

Then in Hot Springs, Arkansas, an assistant principal told me after my presentation about Yaqui that he understood what I was trying to do, and that a presentation like mine probably made sense in "some place like New York." Then he said that he thought I had "exposed the children to more foul language and immorality in the last thirty minutes than some of them had known their whole lives." He said he knew this was so, because one of his own children had been in the audience. I responded by saying that I was very sorry that my program had not met his expectations but that I would love for him to speak to his son about what bullying really looks like at this school. I told him that he might be surprised to find out what kids have to say about bullying when given the chance. A girl standing nearby heard this exchange. When the assistant principal left, she walked up to me. She had her journal with her, and, holding it out to me, she said, "I'm bullied horribly here. This is how I get through my day." We spent a few minutes going through her journal together.

LSM: *You have spoken about "soft censorship." How is soft censorship different?*

MM: Soft censorship is when an obstacle is placed between the reader and a book that someone finds threatening. At a North Carolina school where I was invited to speak, the principal held on to the box of my books that my publisher had sent as presents for the students, keeping them in his office. If a student wanted to read *Yaqui*, I was told, he or she would have to request permission from the principal, who would then decide whether or not the student was "mature enough" to read it. *Yaqui* has been included in displays of books but carefully positioned so that it can't be seen. It has been conveniently left off lists of my books. It's really a very subtle knifing!

Like that principal in North Carolina, some librarians feel they should be the ones to select which kids can read my book. These people are convinced that they are protecting kids. We spend so much time urging children to trust us to help them with their problems. Yet we don't even have the courage to let them read books in which those problems are named for what they are, or to let them freely talk about those problems. So the question I have is this: Why *should* children trust us? That's the part that I think the censors have not thought through carefully.

Soft censorship is especially hard to track, because you can't be everywhere around the country seeing where the book is on the shelf and who's got to bring a permission slip to read it and so on. Then you hear anecdotally comments like, "We can't order the book, because we have a filter on our ordering system that filters out bad language in the title of a book."

LSM: *In* Merci Suárez, *it is Merci's grandmother, who is a very loving character, who says that children don't need to hear about life's ugliness, that there is plenty of time for that later. You leave it to Merci to realize on her own that that is not necessarily so.*

MM: Yes, I wrote it that way because adults spend so much time agonizing over how to protect children from life. People get sick. People die. Hard things happen, and kids are there to see it. There's no way to keep that from happening. I gave that line to Abuela because she adores Merci and I wanted to show that the people who try to censor don't hate children and are not evil. In their minds they are protecting children. They are doing it from a place of love. It's just that it doesn't work, because children actually participate in this mess called living. The best we can do is walk alongside them. But we can't hide things from them.

When it comes to formal challenges to books, the problem is not that parents don't have the right to be involved in deciding what their children read. The problem is that they don't have the right to make that determination for other people's children.

LSM: *How does all this affect you personally?*

MM: Some writers say, "Fine. Challenge me! I'll sell more copies."

Especially YA authors who revel in the feeling of being in your face and standing up to authority. For me, honestly, my first reaction is to sigh, and then I feel a little embarrassed. I raised three children. I think I was and am a good mother. For ten years I was a teacher who really loved and cared about her students. I write books from the most honest place I can, and I always come to it with the thought that childhood is a sacred time, and that I want to honor it in my writing. So when somebody feels that my work is crude or that it in some way harms children or that it brings to them something that is vulgar or detrimental to their moral character, I feel embarrassed and incredibly frustrated that that person cannot see the larger impact of the work.

LSM: *The impact of a challenge often seems to fall most directly on the shoulders of teachers and librarians.*

MM: Yes, and I always feel bad for them as well. To face a challenge even in the best of circumstances, when a formal procedure is in place, takes so much time and causes so much stress and entails a mountain of paperwork. A librarian or teacher can simply pick another book that is not going to cause a headache. So I very much appreciate that they pick mine. When I become aware of a challenge, I reach out to the librarian or principal and offer to be supportive in any way I can. I'm willing to talk to a parent group, write a letter—anything that makes it easier.

LSM: *Why do you think that some of your books have been lightning rods for challenges?*

MM: Some of the censorship has been for the use of the word *ass*. But it's also indirectly censorship around issues of "girl space." How do we bully girls? We call them sluts. We call them hoes. We call them bitches. We use language like that, which is derogatory and sexually charged. When we don't allow discussion of any of that in books, there's a silencing of a discussion that we need to be having. Increasingly, my books deal with immigrant families—all types of immigrant families, documented and undocumented.

It's all there, even in a picture book like *Tía Isa Wants a Car*, in which the girl's parents are living in another country and she is here living with her aunt and uncle and sending back remittances. I'm writing at a time when so many family situations have become politicized and when there are so many reasons for someone to say, "I'm not going to teach that book. I'm not going to have that book in my classroom or library because it's 'anti-American.'" My work opens itself up to all kinds of censorship. But all the art forms, in some way, are about coming out and saying the unsayable, whether it's the word *ass* or the wisecrack "this city sucks." Or whatever it is.

LESLÉA NEWMAN

Born 1955, Brooklyn, New York

"'Did you ever expect your book to cause so much controversy?' is the question I am most frequently asked when the discovery is made: I am the author of the famous/infamous children's book *Heather Has Two Mommies.*"

Born and raised in and around New York, Lesléa Newman attended the University of Vermont, then headed west for studies at the Naropa Institute, an exciting countercultural hot spot in Boulder, Colorado, where she apprenticed with poet Allen Ginsberg. At that time, Newman was an aspiring poet and fiction writer and had given no thought to writing for young people. The story that became *Heather,* her first picture book, grew out of a chance encounter back east a few years later with a lesbian mother who spoke of the need for picture books that reflected her nontraditional family's experience. "Someone should write one," the acquaintance told Newman, whose work she admired. Newman took the comment as an assignment. By the late 1980s, the advent of personal computers had presented authors with new options for publishing their work. *Heather* first appeared in a locally printed, small-press edition funded by an early effort at crowdsourcing. When, a year or so later, an established publisher of gay-and-lesbian-themed books acquired rights to the book, *Heather*'s readership skyrocketed. It soon also became a target for would-be censors. "[*Heather*] brought to the forefront the issues, the conflicts, over what materials concerning GLBT identity [and] lifestyles should be available to young kids," the American Library Association's Deborah Caldwell-Stone told the Associated Press in 2015, at the time of *Heather*'s twenty-fifth anniversary. Its publication coincided, she recalled, with "a time when we were really first acknowledging what we call the culture wars now." Over the years, as the issues and conflicts affecting the LGBTQ community changed, the text and illustrations of the more recent editions of *Heather* changed, too.

The ninth-most frequently challenged book of the 1990s, *Heather Has Two Mommies* went on to become a pop cultural point of reference on television shows as varied as *Will and Grace*, *Gilmore Girls*, *The Daily Show*, and *Real Time with Bill Maher*. In 2006, it even inspired an entire *Simpsons* episode: "Bart Has Two Mommies," of course. It has twice appeared as a *New York Times* crossword puzzle clue and was lampooned by Roz Chast in the *New Yorker* in a cartoon depicting an assortment of books about nontraditional families including one titled *Sarah Has Two*

Mommies Who Are Barry Manilow Fans. Dav Pilkey satirized the controversy surrounding *Heather* in *Captain Underpants and the Preposterous Plight of the Purple Potty People* (2006), in a scene in which best pals George and Harold visit an alternate universe where children are encouraged to read banned books and are offered a copy of *Mommy Has Two Heathers.* In 1994, during the US Senate debate about educational funding, *Heather* was read in its entirety into the Congressional Record.

I first met Newman when we took part in Bank Street's 2015 program on banned books, and we have been friends ever since. We recorded this conversation at the New York apartment of our mutual friend the author Susan Kuklin.

———

LEONARD S. MARCUS: *Tell me about writing* Heather Has Two Mommies.

LESLÉA NEWMAN: I don't recall the actual writing of it, but I do remember the story of its germination, what has become something of an urban lesbian myth that is actually true. I was walking down the street in Northampton, Massachusetts, which has a huge LGBTQ population, when a woman I knew stopped me and said, "I don't have a book to read to my daughter about a family like ours. Somebody should write one." Of course, by "somebody," she meant me. I was known then as a poet but had not yet written any children's books. Being a poet, I should have known better, but I had the common misconception *Ah, a children's book. How hard could that be?* I went to the library and took out armloads of picture books and began to read them.

Looking back, I see that the first published version of *Heather* was not all that well written. The book begins, "This is Heather." I would never start a book like that today. I did the best I could at the time without the benefit of working with an editor. Because *Heather* became a phenomenon, I later had the chance to rewrite the text, which made me very glad.

LSM: *Were there any other picture books like* Heather *at the time?*

LN: The two books that were at all like it were both by Jane Severance. *Lots of Mommies* (1983) is about a little girl who lives with her mother and three other women. When Emily, the girl, falls from the monkey bars during her first day of school, all four women come to help her, and one of her schoolmates remarks, "[Emily] does have lots of mommies." Some people have said about this book, "Well, it's obvious they are lesbians." But it's not obvious, not in the same way that in *Heather* it's clear that the two women are a lesbian couple. Jane Severance had previously written another picture book, called *When Megan Went Away* (1979), about a girl who was living with two women before one of them leaves the family unit. I wanted to write a book about a happy, intact family that consisted of two moms and their daughter.

LSM: *How did* Heather *find its readers?*

LN: I started by sending my manuscript to lesbian feminist publishers I had worked with before. They said that children's book buyers were a completely different market, one that they did not know how to reach. So I then tried children's book publishers. But they said the same thing in reverse, about not knowing how to sell to the lesbian community. All except for one editor, who showed interest but said, "Kids know that two moms can't make a baby, so you need to address that question." That is why I added the famous/infamous alternative insemination scene, which in some cases fueled the controversy surrounding *Heather*. Some people thought just from the title that the book was inappropriate for kids; others had no problem with the fact of Heather having two moms, but felt the explanation of her conception stopped the book from being "child-friendly." I had put the scene in on the advice of that hotshot editor, who ended up rejecting *Heather* anyway. Later, for the tenth-anniversary edition of *Heather*, I took the scene out, having never been 100 percent convinced it was needed.

Finally, inspired by my grandmother, who came from the old country, lived to be ninety-nine, and said, "Just because they say no to me, do you think I'm finished?" I found another way to bring *Heather* into the world. My friend Tzivia Gover and I decided to copublish *Heather*. At the time, Tzivia was a lesbian mom with a one-year-old daughter, and she had a small desktop-publishing business that published mostly pamphlets. To finance the project, we first sent out a fundraising letter, asking people for ten dollars, in return for which they would receive either a copy of the book or a refund in one year's time. We found an illustrator through the lesbian grapevine, then a printer and a distributor. Our edition of *Heather* was ready in December of 1989. Soon lesbian bookstores heard about the book and began placing orders. Then an indie publisher named Sasha Alyson, who had just published Michael

Willhoite's *Daddy's Roommate*, saw *Heather* in a bookstore, contacted me, and said, "We should join forces." He bought out our inventory and became *Heather's* publisher in the spring of 1990.

LSM: *What happened next?*

LN: The first indication that *Heather* was going to have a greater impact than I had imagined came in 1992 when it was mentioned in *Newsweek* in an article about the changing face of the American family. Things went wild after that. A newspaper in Italy picked up on *Heather*, and lots of other publicity followed.

The New York City school system had recently adopted its Children of the Rainbow curriculum, designed to promote tolerance and diversity among elementary school children. Both *Heather* and *Daddy's Roommate* were among the recommended books. A local school board member in Queens named Mary Cummins got hysterical over the books and, in her own words, vowed to "wage war" to have them removed from the list. She used a divide-and-conquer strategy, appealing to the African American and Latinx communities by arguing, "You've wanted a multicultural curriculum for years, and now the gays are destroying it." She was very successful. New York City schools chancellor Joseph Fernandez even received death threats, and he eventually lost his job as a result of the controversy. That was the biggest of the early objections to *Heather*.

LSM: *How did those events affect you personally?*

LN: The most bizarre and unsettling thing that happened was that I received a postcard, sent to me care of my publisher, on the front side of which was this really gross, disgusting, bloody picture of a botched abortion. The unsigned, typewritten message on the back read: "I am Baby Nobody. I wish I could have come into this world. I wouldn't care if I had two mommies or two daddies. I just wanted to be born." The card was postmarked Oregon, but that's all I know about where it came from.

Then because of having my book included in the Children of the Rainbow curriculum, I was invited to be a guest on *The Montel Williams Show*, which I naively thought would be good publicity for the book. I went with a friend to the television studio, and once I had been shown to the greenroom, one of the staffers asked my friend if she was for or against books like mine. She realized right away that they were dividing the audience into two opposing camps, with a view to maximizing an atmosphere of controversy. I had been told by the producer that the show was very supportive of my book, and in the greenroom I met a lovely family with two dads and their kids, so I thought all was well. Little did I know that there was *another* greenroom, where the people on the other side of the debate were waiting. The show turned into something of a prizefight. At the last minute, they decided to seat me in the audience rather than onstage and said that Montel Williams would introduce me and have me say a few words. After the show, as we were leaving, an actual fistfight did break out in the lobby, and I had to be whisked away through a side door by security. It was horrifying.

LSM: *Did being the author of* Heather *make you more of an activist than you were already?*

LN: Absolutely. Before then, I thought of myself as a poet, and not so much as an activist. But when people started asking me to give talks, I thought, *If I'm not going to go out there and defend my book, who will?* I developed a presentation called "Heather's Mommy Speaks Out: Homophobia, Censorship, and Family Values." My first invitation came from a librarians' conference. I spoke at schools, libraries, LGBTQ community centers—whoever wanted me. I did that for a really long time.

LSM: *What were your audiences like?*

LN: Whenever I spoke at a college, the members of the LGBTQ student group would come. I would always offer to have dinner with them before the program to give them a chance to get to know me in an informal setting. Some professors would require their students to attend my talk, with the result that I might have a mixed group, meaning students who were really happy to be there and students who were really unhappy to be there. Sometimes members of the local community would come, too, including people with an agenda, such as the ones who would stand up during the Q and A session and recite chapter and verse from the Bible. I learned to respond to them by interrupting them and saying: "Thank you very much, sir, but do you have an actual question?"

But sometimes people surprise you. Once, at a community center near Albany, New York, I gave my presentation about

Heather, and during the Q and A session, a gentleman in a suit stood up who was holding a thick book that looked suspiciously like a Bible. I thought, *Okay, here we go, he's going to quote from Leviticus.* So I'm mentally preparing for that, but instead he actually does ask a question. He says, "Has anyone ever come to your presentations who strongly opposed your views on lesbian and gay families and afterward changed their mind?" I thought for a moment and said, "Not that I know of." To which he responded: "Well, now one person has."

At colleges I would speak to students who were taking courses in children's literature, sociology, women's studies, and, later, LGBTQ studies. One professor told me that his students had said they didn't want to come to my lecture because people would think they were gay. At one talk in Kansas, Fred Phelps, a notorious antigay Baptist minister, and his gang showed up to stage a protest. At another program, I noticed that people outside were giving out brochures with pink triangles on the cover. I thought, *Great, the gay club is here!* But in fact it was an antigay group that was using the pink triangle symbol to trick people into opening the brochure.

LSM: *How did you talk to grade-school children about* Heather?

LN: To this day, I have never been invited by an elementary school to talk about *Heather*. I was never asked to speak at a high school, either, until I wrote *October Mourning: A Song for Matthew Shepard*. Once, though, I did have an interesting experience at a school where I'd gone to speak about my children's books about animals—you know, my harmless books. As soon as I arrived at

the school, I was called into the principal's office. It was like a flash-back to when I was in high school and always getting into trouble. The principal sat me down and said, "You are *not* to discuss *Heather Has Two Mommies*." I guess he hadn't done his home-work before inviting me. Perhaps a parent had warned him at the last minute. I replied, "I'm here to give a talk about my children's books about animals, and I don't plan on mentioning *Heather*. But if someone asks about *Heather*, I'm not going to pretend I did not write it." I said, "I'm here now, and you can either pay me and send me on my way, or you can allow me to speak. It's your choice. But you cannot censor me." He decided finally to let me speak, but he sat in on every presentation. And wouldn't you know it that at one of the talks a little girl spoke up and said, "I have two mommies—and you wrote my favorite book, *Heather Has Two Mommies!*"
To which I replied, "Yes, I did."

LSM: *You earned your money that day.*

LN: I was furious. I now have a legally binding contract for school visits that states that if my visit is canceled for any reason other than weather or some other act of God, I am entitled to payment.

LSM: *Have you ever censored yourself?*

LN: That's a complicated question. When my book *Ketzel, the Cat Who Composed* was about to come out, the flap copy that my publisher sent me to look over said "by the author of *Heather Has Two Mommies*." I'm not sure if it would be considered self-censorship or not, but I recall thinking, *That's not the most appropriate title* to refer to on this book jacket. I'd rather have Ketzel *be grouped with my other books about animals.* So we edited out the reference to *Heather*. That was purely a marketing decision. I did what I thought was best for that particular book. But I would never stop myself from writing anything.

For a long time, I was adamant that only lesbian and gay people could write authentically about the lesbian and gay experience. But then I read the short story "Brokeback Mountain" by Annie Proulx and was flabbergasted that a straight woman could have written the most beautiful, powerful, and authentic story about gay experience that I had ever read. It changed my mind about what was possible. As I wrote *Hachiko Waits*, a children's historical novel about a very famous and heroic dog who lived in Japan from 1923 to 1935, I struggled with the question of whether I, as a non-Japanese person, had the right to tell this story. I did a lot of homework to get the details right and wrote something like twenty-five drafts. When a Japanese friend who helped me with the research read the final draft, I was so relieved when she said, with tears in her eyes, "You have given me back my childhood."

LSM: *Tell me about some of the other public attacks on* Heather.

LN: In 1992, an antigay activist named Lon Mabon and his organization, the Oregon Citizens Alliance, campaigned for an Oregon statewide ballot proposition known as Measure 9, which would have legalized various forms of discrimination against gay men and lesbians. During their rallies, his group passed around copies of *Heather* and *Daddy's Roommate* as evidence of the "militant homosexual agenda" they opposed, and he personally paraded around at demonstrations, holding up a placard-size blowup of the cover of *Heather*. Happily, Oregon Ballot Measure 9 failed.

Two years later, *Heather* was read on the floor of the US Senate by Senator Bob Smith of New Hampshire, who, along with Jesse Helms of North Carolina, cosponsored an amendment to the annual education appropriations bill that came to be known as the "No Promo Homo" amendment. The stated purpose of the amendment, which the Senate approved by a vote of 63–36 but which was later eliminated, was to bar federal aid to school districts that "carry out a program or activity that has either the purpose or effect of encouraging or supporting homosexuality as a positive lifestyle alternative."

Then, in 1998, in Wichita Falls, Texas, a library patron got so upset that her local library had *Heather* and *Daddy's Roommate* on its shelves that she checked both books out and brought them to her minister, who refused to return them. He tried instead to give the library a check to cover the cost of the two books, which of course the library did not accept. His argument was that taxpayer dollars should not be spent on books like these—as if LGBTQ people don't pay taxes, too. The minister then ran for mayor and used the incident as the basis for his platform. After that, the whole town got caught up in the controversy. Opponents of the books formed prayer circles inside the library and had to be told to leave. Angry letters to the editor appeared in the local newspaper. It got wild. The city council voted to move the books from the children's section of the library to the adult section. Then a petition was circulated that resulted in the two books being isolated in a special section all their own. You had to be at least eighteen years old to check out any book in this special section, which contained only the two children's books *Heather Has Two Mommies* and *Daddy's Roommate*, which was absolutely ridiculous. The ACLU brought a lawsuit against the library, the upshot of which was that the books were permanently returned to the children's section. During the months that this dragged on, the library received about twenty-five donated replacement copies of *Heather*. By then the situation had gotten so ugly that it tore the community apart.

LSM: *How did you know this was happening?*

LN: I first heard about it from my publisher. Later, I was asked to join the lawsuit that was brought by the ACLU as well as a community group called the Wichita Falls Coalition for Free Speech and nineteen local residents who also joined the suit. I decided not to do so after being told that I might have to go to Texas at a moment's notice to testify. Instead, I gave an affidavit that was read in court in which I stated that I had written *Heather* as a children's book, that the Library of Congress had classified it as a children's book, and that I knew it to be shelved in the children's books sections of bookstores and libraries all around the country.

LSM: *How did that experience, and others like it, make you feel?*

LN: Mostly I felt bad for the local children who had two dads or two moms and had to witness this in their town. When do you tell a child, "There are people out there who hate us"? I'm thinking, as a Jew, *When did my parents tell me about anti-Semitism?* I don't remember a time when we sat down and discussed this, but it feels like I always knew there were people who hated my family just because of who we were. After all, I was born a mere ten years after World War II ended, and my grandparents came to this country to escape pogroms in Europe. Anyway, I am sorry that any child has to grow up knowing that for no reason on earth their family is looked down upon as worthy of scorn or as immoral. It makes me sad and furious and determined to write more books about LGBTQ families, despite some people wishing I would not do so.

LSM: *Tell me more about how* Heather *changed after the first edition.*

LN: In the new Candlewick Press edition, published in 2015, I tightened the text and improved the dialogue. Also, in the original version, Heather cries at story hour when she wonders if she is the only child who is there without a daddy. In the twenty-fifth-anniversary version, I decided she had nothing to cry about, so I took that out. Instead of being upset about this, she is merely curious. Also, in the scene where the children all draw pictures of their families, I added a drawing of a child being raised by grandparents, because that is such a common scenario now. And the illustrations show Heather's classroom as being more diverse, which is more representative of the world we all live in today.

LSM: *How has the world changed around* Heather?

LN: When I wrote the book, in 1988, the marriage equality movement wasn't on anybody's mind. That has made a huge difference, giving

LGBTQ families legal protections we never had before. Also, the current generation of kids has grown up with words like *gay* and *lesbian* and *bisexual* and *transgender* and *queer* just rolling off their tongues. This language is in the newspapers. It's on TV. There are gay/straight alliances and LGBTQ clubs in middle schools. Today it's all part of young people's normal range of experience.

In contrast, the people of my generation were so isolated. I remember very clearly the first time I saw the word *gay* in print. It was in 1969, in an article about the Stonewall Uprising, which had just taken place in Greenwich Village. I was thirteen years old. It was after school, and I was in the living room with my mother, who was reading a newspaper that had the word *gay* printed in big letters in a headline. She seemed very upset, and she suddenly said, "The word *gay* certainly meant something different in *my* time!" I don't think I had ever heard her sound so indignant or disgusted before. I wondered, what could be so upsetting about that article? Later I read it myself. I had no inkling then that I was gay or even what that would mean. I had just always felt different—and doomed to a life of misery.

We had moved from Brooklyn to Long Island when I was eight. I don't remember much from before the move except that Brooklyn was a lot livelier than the suburbs. Growing up, I had a best friend who I was probably in love with, although I would not have had the language to say so. I just knew we were inseparable. I knew early on that I never wanted to be a mother. The other day somebody asked me, "How's your daughter, Heather?" That always makes me laugh. The assumptions people make!

I was smart and read a lot. I wrote poetry from the time I was very young and got attention for doing it. It was always my goal to be a writer. I would look at author photos on the backs of books and imagine my own photo there instead. Although not really a tomboy, I wasn't that feminine, either. In high school, I didn't wear skirts or makeup. I was the class wit, and I used humor to mask my unhappiness.

My first publications were poems published in *Seventeen* magazine when I was a teenager. Once, the poetry editor of *Seventeen* even invited me to her office. I got all dressed up in a black leotard and a wraparound flowered skirt and those black cloth Mary Jane shoes we were all wearing at the time and took the train from Long Island into Manhattan. The editor took me back to her office and very dramatically dumped the contents of two big shopping bags onto her desk: all poetry manuscripts. Then she said: "This is what comes to me in the mail every single day. Your poems stood out like a shining star."

LSM: *You continued to write poetry at college and then as a graduate student at Naropa Institute's colorfully named Jack Kerouac School of Disembodied Poetics, in Boulder, Colorado. While there, you became the assistant to one of your teachers, the great American poet Allen Ginsberg. What did you learn from him?*

LN: Allen, or "Ginzy," as he called himself, was a serious practicing Buddhist. His mantra—"First thought, best thought"—runs through my mind constantly when I write. This, by the way, doesn't mean that the first thing one writes is brilliant and doesn't need

editing! It means that one should constantly remember that first flash of insight that inspired a piece of writing and remain true to it (at least that's my interpretation). I often think of something else Allen said, too: "Writing is 33 percent perspiration, 33 percent respiration, and 33 percent inspiration." To which I replied: "Wait a minute, Allen. I'm the daughter of a certified public accountant. That adds up to only 99 percent. What's the other 1 percent?" He gleefully replied, "Magic!"

LSM: *References to magic are often cited when the Harry Potter books, among others, are challenged. Why do you think some people feel the impulse to challenge and ban books? What do you imagine goes through their minds?*

LN: It's often out of fear. The fear is that if a girl reads *Heather*, she's going to become a lesbian. If a boy reads *Sparkle Boy*, he's going to want to wear a dress. But you have to take one step back and ask the people who think this, *Why are you so afraid of having your child be his or her or their authentic self, whatever that self is?* I have two responses to people who want to ban books. The first is that as a child I read literally thousands of books about straight people, and not one of them changed my sexuality. My second response is: Don't you want your child to be happy?

Many parents have a preconceived notion of how they want their child to be. In my own parents' case, their vision for me was to be straight, to marry a nice Jewish boy, and have 3.2 children. Such preconceived notions often come with the fear that if the child finds out there are other ways of being in the world, he or she or they might choose to live that other way. Which isn't exactly how it works.

I gave a reading at a university in North Dakota where the head of the school's LGBTQ student group was openly gay and wonderfully flamboyant. He told me he had grown up on a farm, never met a drag queen, and had never been exposed to any kind of gay culture. Then one day when he was eight years old, Marilyn Monroe appeared on TV in *Some Like It Hot*. He took one look at her and said to himself, *That's who I want to be!* Where, he asked, does an idea like that come from? Then he said: "I knew in that moment that my whole world had opened up for me, and I knew that that was who I am."

You can't stop the rain. Tragically, some young people who do get stopped from being themselves commit suicide. My parents took a while, but they came around when they finally realized that coming out had made me so much happier. I think in the end that that is what all parents want for their child.

LSM: *You have said that the people who challenge books attribute a kind of power to books that they don't really have. What power do books have?*

LN: With *Heather*, I went from licking envelopes and begging people for a ten-dollar bill to having my story read into the Congressional Record. I could never have imagined that happening. A book cannot change the inner core of who you are. It can't alter what you came with down the birth canal and into this world. But a book can validate, comfort, educate, and enlighten. Books can help make this a more accepting, respectful, and more celebratory world.

KATHERINE PATERSON

Born 1932, Huai'an, China

For a daughter of Presbyterian missionaries who grew up to become a missionary herself, Katherine Paterson has gotten herself into a surprising lot of trouble. It is true that she has long been regarded as one of the children's book world's finest contemporary novelists; and that a spectacular collection of honors have come her way, including two Newbery Medals, two National Book Awards, and the international Hans Christian Andersen Award and Astrid Lindgren Memorial Award, among others; and that the Library of Congress declared her a Living Legend and appointed her its second National Ambassador for Young

People's Literature. Yet it is also the case that Paterson's best-known books, *Bridge to Terabithia* (1977), *The Great Gilly Hopkins* (1978), and *Jacob Have I Loved* (1980), have all drawn repeated challenges by parents, self-appointed moralists, and others for whom the author's language or subject matter or irreverent attitude touched a nerve.

It is Paterson's pursuit of one of her most deeply held ideals as a writer—her unswerving commitment to psychological truth-telling— that has so often upset her critics. The sudden, accidental death of a twelve-year-old's best friend. The raw language of an enraged, long-neglected foster child. The bitterness of sibling strife. Paterson has examined these and other emotionally intense, morally difficult matters in vivid, tautly crafted stories that feel both matter-of-fact and revelatory. The American Library Association highlighted this aspect of her work when it conferred its lifetime achievement award on her in 2013. The citation read in part: "Paterson's unflinching yet redemptive treatment of tragedy and loss helped pave the way for ever more realistic writing for young people."

As one of the children's book world's most visible figures, Paterson has had occasion to comment publicly on book banners' efforts, and has challenged the notion that writing like hers, which aims for an unvarnished version of the truth about growing up, could ever be in conflict with religious faith. "The fact that I call myself a Christian and see my work as a calling from God does not make people who wish to ban my books very happy," she told an audience in 1998. "Nor could I succeed in explaining to them my belief that if I tried to write books according to their guidelines, I would be untrue to the gift that God has given me." To further illuminate her point, Paterson quoted the American writer

Flannery O'Connor, who, she noted, was also a devoutly religious person: "Fiction is about everything human and we are made out of dust, and if you scorn getting yourself dusty, then you shouldn't write fiction. It isn't grand enough."

Well into the fifth decade of her career, Paterson maintains a prodigious writing and travel schedule. We last crossed paths at a Mexico City literature conference and at the one hundredth birthday party of a mutual friend in New York. She was at home in Brattleboro, Vermont, when we talked by phone for this interview.

———

LEONARD S. MARCUS: *You have said you were both a shy child and a show-off. How did those two opposing traits coexist in you?*

KATHERINE PATERSON: As I have gotten older and known more people who are entertainers of one kind or another, I've realized that this is characteristic of entertainers. They love to entertain an audience but find it difficult to meet people one-on-one. I remember my sister saying to me once before a speech I was to give, "Well, how many people are going to be in the audience?" I said, "I don't know, maybe a thousand, two thousand." She said, "What?!" To which I replied, "Better two thousand than two!" I used to think that the two worst things in the world were publishers' cocktail parties and church coffee hours, because I'm just not good at making small talk. With age, I have gotten better at it.

LSM: *Were you known to your school friends as a storyteller?*

KP: Sort of, but I never thought of myself then as a writer. I was a reader and therefore a lover of stories. Both my parents were southern, so I grew up hearing stories all the time. My father wasn't as much of a talker as my mother, but I think that Southerners have it in their DNA to tell stories and that everything turns into a story for them.

I never did much writing as a child, and fortunately, the few pieces that I did write have been lost. My first conscious efforts were in elementary school, when I would write plays for my friends and me to act out on the playground. Occasionally the teacher would ask us to perform them in the classroom, too.

LSM: *They can't have been too bad, then! As a novelist, you have always been so skilled at dialogue. Does writing a novel feel at all like writing a play?*

KP: Yes, in some ways it does. I'm writing a novel now, and I'll have a page of nothing but dialogue and say to myself, *Hmm. Maybe I should have some description!* I can always hear the speeches more easily than I can visualize the scenes, which is embarrassing to me because writers are supposed to be so observant.

LSM: *As a young child, you were fluent in both Mandarin and English.*

KP: Yes, not that I can speak Mandarin anymore. Being bilingual as a child does good things for your brain. I found a letter that my father had written to his mother in which he was either appalled or amazed—I could not tell which—that I couldn't be shut up in either language. I was not quite two at the time.

LSM: *You told me once that you were a child performer on radio.*

KP: That was my show-off personality. We were living in Winston-Salem, North Carolina, then, and I was eleven and twelve. Every Saturday morning, the local radio station broadcast a drama, and whenever they needed a girl, they called on me. I loved acting, and I loved being taken seriously as an actor. I would catch the bus and go across town to the station. It was like entering a magic land for me.

I don't remember any of my roles, but I do recall my most celebrated performance. The worst possible sin on radio is dead air. That day, in the middle of the broadcast, I suddenly realized that the man who was playing the father had lost his place in the script. Immediately, I began jabbering away, making up dialogue. Afterward you would have thought I had saved the *Titanic*. The radio people carried on about my quick thinking, and I felt very proud of myself. I kept acting in high school and college.

LSM: Gilly Hopkins *has been criticized for the "bad" words that are a major part of Gilly's vocabulary. Do you remember learning your first curse words?*

KP: Oh, my! In my parents' house, you couldn't even say *darn* or *gee*, because *gee* was short for *Jesus* and *darn* was for *damn*. *Gosh* was for *God*, so you couldn't say that, either. My parents were very strict about language. Years later, I told my own children, "You know, it's all right to know these words, but if you use them all the time, they lose their meaning. There's going to be a time when you really need to cuss, and you'll have used them all up, and they won't have any power for you anymore. So wait until you need them!" Now when I watch a show on cable TV, I think, *Oh, come on. Expand your vocabulary slightly!*

LSM: *You read widely as a child. How did you think about the Bible—the Good Book—in relation to all the other good books you discovered?*

KP: Of course, the Bible was a very important book in my house. We had the King James version, which is so beautiful, and which, I think, does good things for your language. We read the Bible every day at home. I had a terrible temper as a little child. You know, anything to get attention if you are the middle child of five. Good behavior didn't get nearly as much attention as bad behavior! My mother was very distressed by this, so she told me to select my favorite Bible passage and go and read it every time I felt like I was going to fly off the handle. My favorite passage was the thirteenth chapter of First Corinthians, which is all about love. My childhood Bible is tear-stained from all my angry tears.

LSM: *In* Bridge to Terabithia, *you gave Leslie a speech about the Bible that I want to ask you about. She says to Jess: "It's crazy, isn't it? . . . You have to believe it, but you hate it. I don't have to believe it, and I think it's beautiful."*

KP: That's very often the case with people, don't you think? A believer who takes the Bible literally has to try to believe all the very contradictory concepts that sit side by side in it. But someone coming at the Bible fresh will see an enormous amount of beauty.

LSM: *Was that one of the passages that got you into trouble with some of your readers?*

KP: When *Bridge to Terabithia* was published, I began to get a lot of reviews like the one that referred to the "gutter and unholy language" in the book. When I showed the review to my son, John, who was about twelve at the time, he said, "I'll give her some 'gutter and unholy language'!" You know, it's a little absurd when you look at it. Jess says *Lord* a lot, as people in the South do, sort of as punctuation. That's not "gutter and unholy" language. Maybe *hell* and *damn* are unholy, but they're not what I would consider "gutter language." I tried to use those words when I needed that kind of powerful cussing, and of course, in *Gilly Hopkins* when it occurs, it's because a child like that, as I've often said, is not going to say *fiddlesticks* when she's angry.

LSM: *Do you recall anything more about that review?*

KP: It was written by a schoolteacher, and because her name and a way to contact her were provided in the review, I wrote to her. I have tried to respond to the people who criticized my books if they weren't totally crazy, because I figured they were sincere and deserved an answer. I wrote to her and tried to explain why I had used the words that I did. I said, "I'm not expecting you to agree with me, but I am sorry you were offended." I got a letter back from her in which she said how grateful she was that I had taken her feelings seriously. She said she hadn't thought anybody would understand what she meant. To me, that made it worth it. I felt that woman was sincere—and worried—and didn't want me to be a bad influence on my young readers.

On the other hand, if someone is absolutely crazy, you're just handing them more ammunition if you write them back. I heard of a minister who said that he was making it his "mission in life" to get *Bridge to Terabithia* off the shelves of every library in every school. I thought, *Man, get yourself a larger mission!* If I may judge—which I'm not allowed to do, actually—I would say that somebody like that just wants power, as opposed to the parent whose aim is to protect.

I gave a talk about *Gilly Hopkins* to a class of schoolchildren, and a little boy got up and said, "Why do you use bad words in books? Aren't you scared that kids will read those words and think they should use them, too?" I said, "Well, now, Gilly lies, and steals, and has terrible prejudice against African American people. Now, does that make you want to lie and steal and have terrible prejudice?" He said, "Oh, no!" And I said, "Well, then, I'm not sure why you think the words she says are going to make you imitate them, because you're not going to imitate anything else that she's doing." He kind of looked at me, and said, "Oh . . . yeah." In cases like that, I never know what parent or teacher may have prompted the child to ask the question.

I try very hard when I go to schools to speak to one class at a time, because I find that I like to have a real dialogue with the kids. It makes for a much healthier atmosphere than there would be if I were speaking to a huge group. This way, I'm not an entertainer. I'm just someone else who loves books.

LSM: Bridge to Terabithia *has also been challenged over concerns that children might have a hard time handling a story about the death of a child. How was the subject of death treated in your family?*

KP: It wasn't hidden. We lived in China through war and famine. As a child, I saw an awful lot of death and was truly terrified by it.

As a writer for children, you're struggling with the demons of your own childhood, and while I was writing *Bridge to Terabithia*, Jess's fear was very real to me. I remember a child I had known who died accidentally and tragically in our church in Winston-Salem, and when my parents were going to visit the family and, I think, also the body of the child, they asked me if I wanted to go, too. I was terrified at the thought of seeing her dead and refused. They didn't force me, but they gave me the opportunity. I also remember that when my dog was killed accidentally, I didn't want to see it, either. My father thought I surely would want to see my dead dog, but I didn't, and he didn't push it.

LSM: *Did you have an experience while growing up that made you feel that you were not a child anymore?*

KP: Oh, that's interesting. . . . My parents always treated me with a lot of respect and let me make choices, so there was never a time when I broke loose and rebelled. When I was in college, I had a chance to go to England one summer. I had enough money to pay for my transportation, and I was going to be living with someone who would feed me. So I told my parents that this was what I was planning to do, and it never occurred to me that they would try to stop me. My classmates were so surprised that my parents would let me go. I was very fortunate in my parents. Later, as a missionary in my twenties, I lived for a time in Japan, and when I returned to America I felt so different from the people here. My mother was appalled at the clothes I was wearing, which were certainly not in good shape, let alone stylish. When she wanted to buy me new clothes, I rebelled at the thought of that, and I thought that I was finally having my adolescent rebellion.

LSM: *You've described being a child in China and watching as the occupying Japanese troops practiced on the beach for a possible future invasion of San Francisco. Experiences like that one must have had a big impact on you and your understanding of what people were capable of doing.*

KP: Yes, and when our family came back to the States from China, it was very apparent to me that everyone regarded me as extremely weird. So I didn't share experiences like that with them. I was desperate to fit in and to be regarded as normal. It took me a long time to realize that I wasn't like anybody else, because nobody is like anybody else. There was no point trying to fit myself into a mold that was not going to be helpful in any way.

LSM: *You've said that when you were preparing to go to Japan as a missionary, one of the hardest things you had to do was overcome your hatred of Japan, given the extreme brutality of the Japanese army that you had witnessed in China.*

KP: I've said and probably written before that to have the experience of being loved by people you thought you hated is something that everybody should experience. There's nothing quite like it. While I was in Japan as a missionary, the Japanese were so loving and so caring toward me. I was given so much. Part of it was because I was single, and they thought that meant my parents didn't really care about me, that they had let me go to Japan without first having gotten me a good husband. It didn't matter how much I explained to them that that's not the way we did it in America. They felt very protective toward me, especially when I lived in the countryside and there were no other English-speaking people close by.

LSM: *The same pattern comes up over and over in your books. In* Gilly Hopkins *and* Park's Quest, *for example, the main character is deeply suspicious at first of a stranger, and then things change for the better between them.*

KP: I remember that when I was first thinking about writing for children, and trying to learn to write, and reading books about how to do it, one of the cardinal rules seemed to be that the child protagonist has to solve his or her own problem. I thought, *That's nonsense! Children are powerless.* I know, and I've learned, and I've been taught over and over and over again, that unless a child has one caring adult in his or her life, there's not much chance that they are going to grow up to be a loving, caring person. There's got to be somebody—if it's not the parents, it's got to be a teacher or a friend or a relative—who lets them know they're loved and how important they are.

LSM: *Do you think a book can do that for a child?*

KP: A book might help but somebody will have to find that book and give it to the child.

LSM: *How did you come to write* The Great Gilly Hopkins?

KP: There was a long time when the only thing I knew about the book was that I wanted to write about a character named Galadriel Hopkins, and I didn't know why that was going to be her name. My husband and I had been asked to be foster parents, and afterward, I realized I hadn't done a very good job of it. Because I knew it was temporary, I had treated these boys as if they were Kleenex. I realized how awful it would be if a child felt that the world considered him or her disposable. So when I was writing *Gilly*, I decided I would give her the best foster mother in the world.

LSM: *What books or authors meant the most to you as you were starting out on your writing career?*

KP: By the time I started writing myself, I had read *Charlotte's Web* and realized what respect E. B. White had for children, and how important that was.

LSM: Charlotte's Web *is another book that got into trouble because the heroine dies at the end.*

KP: Well, it's part of life, and if you rehearse it in a book, then you're better prepared when it happens. When people say, "I know this child, and she lost a parent or friend, so I gave her a copy of *Bridge to Terabithia*," I think, *Oh, too late!*—because I don't think a book is a cure, but I do think very often it's a preparation.

LSM: *Some people believe that books have the power to do damage to a child.*

KP: I don't know that I can argue with that, because if a book has power, you really can't control the power. The reception of the power is the reader's choice. I don't think you can decide for another reader what might be damaging for them, and I think most children would stop reading if they realized it was something that was hurting them or if it was something they didn't want to understand.

One mistake that's often made with *Bridge* is thinking that a child who is a good, proficient reader is also necessarily emotionally ready for it. I've had parents brag to me that their third grader had read *Jacob Have I Loved*, and I think, *Hmm. That's very interesting but it's certainly not a book that I would give to an eight-year-old.* I think that up to a certain point, children need to have happy endings. By the time they're nine or ten, children of intelligence are looking around and realizing that the world is not all happily-ever-after. That is when they're going to be ready for a book that mirrors the reality of what they're learning life is about.

LSM: *Tell me more about the book challenges you have experienced over the years.*

KP: Challenges would come from different directions. Sometimes I would hear directly from a teacher or librarian who was facing a challenge. In that case, I would immediately put them in touch with the American Library Association and the other organizations that I knew could give them professional help and advice. I think by and large my publishers tried to protect me from news of the latest challenges, but they would send me letters that had come in the mail to me, or somebody would see a headline in a local newspaper and send me the information. I would try to respond if I knew someone was under siege and say, "How can I help?"

In 1983, there was a famous case in Salina, Kansas, involving *Gilly Hopkins*. The school librarian there, who was the only African American staff member at the school, was in touch with me with updates daily. After a parent complained about the book, the school principal had told her to take *Gilly Hopkins* off the shelves. The librarian refused, saying to the principal that if she took every book off the shelves that *some* parent was offended by, there would be very little left. To prove her point, she then began pulling books right and left off the shelves and placing them on a cart. When she pulled a copy of the Bible—which certainly plenty of people *have* been offended by—the principal screamed! So then the principal brought the matter before the school board. The afternoon that the board convened to discuss my book and this librarian's "insubordination," I was at our local high school swim meet, where one of my children was competing. I could hardly wait to get home to find out what happened.

What happened was that some member of the school board had insisted that every single member of the board read the book. At the meeting, the board totally exonerated the librarian and said they felt that my book was probably very helpful for the kids. In the end, the librarian left her job after that year anyway, because it was just too uncomfortable to try to carry on with the same principal still in charge. She became a librarian at Lincoln University. We still correspond now and then and have even gotten together twice. It made for a very nice friendship! But every time one of these cases would come up, some librarian or teacher would be in trouble because of me. Librarians like her would risk their entire careers.

LSM: *Do you think that challenges like the one you just described have any impact on you as a writer?*

KP: Apparently I have not changed, because I am still writing books that offend some people. I have discovered that the better a book sells and the more often it's used in schools, the more often it is going to be challenged.

LSM: *You predicted in one of your speeches that the end of the Cold War might result in more book challenges and censorship here. What did you mean by that?*

KP: When the Berlin Wall fell and Communism seemed to be on the wane, I turned to my husband and said half in jest, "Now they'll start coming after me." He didn't know what I was talking about, so I explained, "There are people who have to have an enemy." For a while after that, I *did* see more challenges to my books.

LSM: *You've said that the difficulty you had in writing about Leslie's death had as much to do with your own feelings about mortality as they did with your concern for children's feelings. Do you think that the adults who have objected to your book were and are projecting their own fears?*

KP: Oh, yes. I think that's likely. It was interesting how few of the objections were directly about the death. I remember one objection that did say that death was not an appropriate subject for ten-year-olds. I thought, *Well, two of my children have lost friends in childhood.* One was eight, and the other was in preschool when it happened. It's not what we would wish for children, but it happens. More often, though, the objections to *Terabithia* have been about the language, and one that I recall objected to the "incest" in the novel. That one puzzled me. I said to my friend Stephanie, "I get the objections to death and to the language, but I don't get the incest." She said, "Katherine, the brother and sister slept in the same bedroom!" To which I replied, "Don't they know any poor people?"

LSM: *Early in the book, you write: "Jess drew the way some people drink whiskey." I read that and thought,* Katherine is throwing a grenade! *Of all things to compare drawing with. You were putting the reader on notice, weren't you?*

KP: That's right, as in: stop now if you're easily offended.

LSM: *I'm fascinated by the dreamlike golden room that Leslie's father creates in their house. Why did you feel that image belonged in the story?*

KP: One reason I won't teach writing is that so much of my writing is instinctual, not deliberate or planned. But I think, looking back on it, that I'm building up to a sort of wonderful, wonderful life that's going to get snatched away, and the more beautiful that life is, the more wrenching the loss of it is. Don't you think?

For me, the most powerful scene in the book is when Jess's father comes to the stream where Jess has thrown the paints into the water and comforts him. His father loves him, but until then Jess did not truly know it. When I was in Hollywood for the movie premiere, I saw Robert Patrick, who played Jess's father, and went over to him and just threw my arms around him. Of course, he didn't know me from a hole in the wall, so that night at the party the director gave, I apologized to him for having tried to hug him. I told him he had done such a beautiful job with that scene, and he forgave me!

LSM: *Some readers of* Jacob Have I Loved *must have objected to your blunt account of Louise's hateful feelings toward her sister.*

KP: Yes, of course. But, let's face it. I don't know why we're so afraid of true feelings in our children when we know perfectly well we had those feelings ourselves, and maybe still have them. When I was writing the book, I thought I was writing about other people's jealousies. But when I reread it later, I got so angry, I realized, *Oops! I don't think this is somebody else's problem.*

LSM: *Did you have the title in mind from the beginning?*

KP: Yes, because I was deliberately writing the Jacob and Esau story. But I didn't think my publisher would let me keep the title. Of course, in the Bible, Esau turns out to be a much nicer person than Jacob, and when I was doing the research for the book, I found that wonderful quote from the Old Testament commentary called the Midrash, which says that the Messiah will not come until the tears of Esau cease to flow.

LSM: *It's one of the ultimate stories about loving thine enemy.*

KP: After the book came out here, my British publisher called me long-distance and said she wanted to lop off the last chapter. I said, "I don't mind if you don't publish the book in England. But if you do publish it, it has to have that chapter." I named it *Jacob Have I Loved*, so "Esau" *has* to love "Jacob" before it's over.

LSM: *Louise decides she wants to become a doctor, but then, when she is discouraged from doing so, she accepts the opinions of others and instead trains to be a nurse-midwife. Why did you downsize Louise's dream? Was it to give a truer reflection of the time in which the story is set?*

KP: Absolutely. With all those soldiers coming home from war and going to medical school, there wasn't going to be a place for someone like Louise. As a nurse-midwife, she became more of a doctor than any doctor you know. She was doing it all. But I've gotten criticism on this part of the story, too. It's very interesting to me that people really want to impose twenty-first-century values on a different century and will get mad at the writer for not doing so. You want us to be truthful, but you don't want us to mess with your notions about what's right.

LSM: *You seem to enjoy researching your books.*

KP: Yes, I do, and I can't think of a book that hasn't demanded research of some sort, even *Bridge to Terabithia*. I had first seen the Sacred Grove I described in the Adirondacks, and I wanted to put it in the book, but I didn't know if such a thing would work in a story set in Virginia. So I had to call up someone at the US Forest Service and explain that I had put a mixed woods next to a pine forest, and could that really occur in Virginia? He said it was unusual, but it *was* possible. I said, "*Possible* is all I need!"

LSM: *Research is related to empathy in that it is all about getting out of yourself and into the backstories of your characters.*

KP: That's right. In writing a novel, you start wherever you can. I usually try to know where I'm aiming before I start writing. By the time I finish the first draft, I know so much more about my characters than I did when I started that I am ready to go back and say, "Well, they certainly wouldn't have done *that*." Or, "They wouldn't have done it that way." Or, "They would never have said that. Not under those circumstances." My feeling is that the reason you rewrite is to find out who these people, your characters, truly are.

LSM: *Have you tried to imagine your way into the minds of the people who have objected to your books?*

KP: Yes, I have. I've decided that very often it is someone who sincerely wants to protect innocence. The fact that I'm not sure how much you really can protect innocence makes me the writer I am rather than the parent or teacher or guardian that they are.

DAV PILKEY
Born 1966, Cleveland, Ohio

"I guess I really shouldn't be surprised that my Captain
Underpants series continues to top banned-books lists," Dav Pilkey told
the *Guardian* in 2015, around the time that work was getting underway
on DreamWorks Pictures' first animated film based on the books. After
all, Pilkey recalled, he was barely old enough to read and write when
he had his first close encounter with an outraged reader. It happened at
school, in North Ridgeville, Ohio, where, as a seven-year-old faced with
the inability of his teachers to cope with a child with dyslexia and ADHD
(Attention Deficit Hyperactivity Disorder), he discovered cartooning as
a private escape, a creative outlet, and a social calling card all rolled into

one. His classmates were charmed by his efforts, but that was not true for those in charge of his education. "My very first Captain Underpants stories were 'banned' by my second-grade teacher. She took things a step further by actually ripping my pencil-drawn comics to shreds, telling me that I couldn't spend the rest of my life making silly books. Fortunately I was not a very good listener."

Pilkey majored in English in college and might have become a teacher himself had not one of his professors told him that he had the right combination of talents for a career as a children's book author and illustrator. Winning a national student writing contest resulted in the publication in 1987 of his first book, an illustrated fable about the arms race called *World War Won*. Over the next ten years, he gradually built his reputation with a number of stand-alone books while also experiencing his fair share of rejection. Then in 1997 came Captain Underpants, the series that made him one of the world's most widely read children's author-illustrators. More than eighty million books from the series have now gone out to readers in more than twenty-five languages. Pilkey's more recent series, Dog Man, which launched in 2016, recounts the adventures of a comic-book character first seen in Captain Underpants, and has proven just as popular with fans.

From childhood, when he loved irreverent humor magazines like *Mad*, Pilkey has always enjoyed a silly sight gag and an outrageous pun. He poked hilarious fun at *Goodnight Moon* in his picture book *The Dumb Bunnies*, and in *The Adventures of Captain Underpants* he cautioned readers with a "Sturgeon General's Warning: Some material in this book may be considered offensive by people who don't wear underwear." For good measure in the latter book, he also red-flagged the novel's "Extremely

Graphic Violence Chapter" (number 16), in which George and Harold fight back against evil robots by hitting their attackers over the head with wooden planks. Young readers got the joke and were wildly entertained, but enough adults have been disturbed by the "offensive language" and "violence" they found in Captain Underpants to secure a place for the series on the American Library Association's annual list of ten most frequently challenged books in 2002, 2004, 2005, 2012, 2013, 2014, and 2018—twice (2013 and 2014) in the number one spot.

Dav Pilkey and I have not met in person, and I was delighted when he agreed to respond by email to my questions for this interview.

LEONARD S. MARCUS: *How much of your childhood self went into the characters of George and Harold?*

DAV PILKEY: At first, George and Harold were completely based on me. George was my wild and crazy side—my extroverted, Freudian id. Harold was my introverted side—the shy, quiet, worried side of me, my superego.

They stayed that way for the first two books, but eventually, after hanging around in my brain for several years, George and Harold began to take on personalities of their own. George evolved into a much smarter person—he's probably a genius. And Harold is more creative and thoughtful—and a much better artist than I was at his age.

LSM: *All kids need to find a way to fit in and function in a world that is not altogether to their liking. How did you go about it?*

DP: My biggest problem as a child was a feeling of isolation. It started around second grade, when I was diagnosed with dyslexia and with "extreme hyperactivity" (what they now call ADHD). My teacher did not have the patience or resources to deal with a child like me, so she often sent me out into the hallway to sit by myself at a desk. This hallway desk followed me from second to fourth grade, and I spent a good deal of time out there every day. Even when I was in the classroom, my desk was often separated from the rest of my classmates, so I couldn't talk to other kids.

I think this is why making comics became such an important part of my life. I wanted to remain relevant. So I would spend my time in the hallway, making up silly characters and writing adventure stories about them. These comic-book adventures (usually just a few pages stapled together) proved to be very popular with my classmates, and my identity began to change. I was no longer the kid who couldn't read very well, or the kid who couldn't control himself. I became the artist. The comic-book kid. The guy who made the funny books.

LSM: *What were you reading when you were the right age to be reading* The Adventures of Captain Underpants?

DP: At that age, I had no interest in "assigned" reading. Anything that was educational seemed like homework and drudgery. I had become one of the "reluctant readers" that educators like to talk about.

The funny thing was, I *liked* to read. I was *always* reading. I usually had my nose in a copy of *Mad* magazine or *Dynamite* magazine, or a joke book, or a collection of *Peanuts* cartoons. My teachers would take these things away from me because they felt that my choices weren't substantial enough, so I reluctantly read (or pretended to read) whatever they gave me instead.

My mom started getting worried. She thought that *what* I was reading might not be as important as everyone else thought it was. She decided to make sure *that* I was reading. She made sure I had *Mad* and *Cracked* magazines, and she always let me pick out whatever I wanted from the Scholastic Book Club flyer. And so, while the rest of the world read *Charlotte's Web*, I read what my teachers referred to as "garbage." That garbage turned me into a reader.

LSM: Mad *was really so sophisticated as well as so much fun.*

DP: *Mad* seemed to embrace its lowbrow status and used it as a format to critique society. There was a lot of very intelligent social and political commentary going on in those seemingly "dumb" pages.

I think my first experience with a banned book was probably my obsession with Maurice Sendak's *Where the Wild Things Are* when I was four years old. My mother did not want me reading the book (she thought it would give me nightmares), so we didn't have it in our house. Fortunately our church had a copy, and I would hide under the desk by the doorway and read it every chance I got. I *loved* the monsters and the way Max's room grew into a jungle. I don't think the book inspired any actual nightmares—just a love of art and of the interaction of words and paintings.

LSM: *I am going to guess that you grew up as a fan of James Marshall*

and Shel Silverstein, and the Rotten Ralph books of Nicole Rubel
and Jack Gantos. Are there children's book people who came before
you whose books have meant a lot to you as an author-artist?

DP: Yes—all of the above, as well as the gentle humor of Arnold Lobel.
Dr. Seuss was also a big influence. These wonderful artists entertained me as a child, and they became my teachers when I began
my career as a children's book author and illustrator.

LSM: All school-aged children go through a period of fascination with
bathroom humor. Can you remember your own experience of this?

DP: I think my love of bathroom humor as a child revolved around
poop and pee, and how important it is to learn to do these things
in a potty, like big people. But once you've mastered the skill,
you're suddenly forbidden from ever mentioning bathroom-related
words again. Those very adults who talked happily and endlessly
about poopies and pee-pee and potties and diapers and underpants suddenly get very upset and offended at the mention of such
things. Many adults go so far as to label normal, healthy, necessary
bodily functions as disgusting and immoral, and kids find this
hilarious. Children laugh because they're discovering the power of
words to shine a light on the hypocrisy of adults.

LSM: Was there a Mr. Krupp—a hostile school principal—in your life
then?

DP: There was a Mr. Krupp in my life as a child. I had a principal in
elementary school, and another one in high school, who seemed
not only to hate children but to thrive on crushing their spirits (or

perhaps it was just *my* spirit getting crushed that delighted them).
Mr. Krupp is a combination of those two principals, as well as a
couple of teachers I had throughout the years. Mr. Krupp's name
actually comes from the name of a crotchety old man in one of
my favorite Hal Roach's Our Gang comedies called *Shrimps for a
Day*. I borrowed the name from that character, but unfortunately
I misremembered the name of "Mr. Krupp." His actual name was
Mr. Crutch.

LSM: *Did making comics at school change the way your teachers saw
you?*

DP: I think comic-making as a child was mostly something that I did
to keep a connection to my classmates. They loved reading my
comics—sometimes they'd even fight over them—and that made
me feel like a part of the group, even when I was separated from
everyone else. Making comic books was also a way to change my
identity in the classroom. I remember my second-grade teacher
liked to humiliate me by threatening to send me back to kindergarten because I couldn't read as well as everyone else. She made
it seem like something she actually *could* do, and I worried about
it a lot. So there was a real danger of being seen as the class baby. I
also received much more than my share of isolation and corporal
punishment, and so the reputation of "bad kid" was never far away,
either. Making comics turned the attention away from those things
and shined a different light on me. I was the classroom artist. The
comic kid. That's how I wanted to be known.

LSM: *Was there a teacher who encouraged you? Did your parents provide that kind of support?*

DP: I had two teachers who changed my life. My kindergarten teacher, Mrs. Krapp (her real name), singled me out as the classroom artist and made a big deal about it. She would often hang my artwork in a special place, like on the classroom door or above the chalkboard, right in the center, so that everybody could see it. Mrs. Krapp made me *feel* like an artist.

Similarly, in college, an English professor made a big deal about an essay I wrote. She made copies of it, passed it around, and spent the rest of the class time reading and championing it. After class, she asked me if I had ever considered writing books for children (she had also admired the cartoony sketches in my notebook). I had never considered it until that moment, and I was so inspired that I started writing my first children's book that week. It would later become my first published book, *World War Won*.

My parents, however, provided the most consistent and enduring support. They always encouraged my drawing and my comic-making, but I think they were concerned that many of my stories were getting torn up by my teachers, and many more were borrowed by friends who often lost them. So when I was in the third or fourth grade, my parents commissioned a special series of comics just for themselves. The only catch was that I wasn't allowed to take them to school. They couldn't leave the house. I was inspired by the challenge and ended up making a twenty-book series of comics for them about a character named Water

Man, which included a few spin-off adventures about secondary characters. Sometime in my twenties, they surprised me by giving all my Water Man comics back to me. I'd almost forgotten about them, but my parents had saved them all and kept them in pristine condition. Most of the comics I made during my childhood didn't survive my childhood, but thanks to my parents, Water Man did.

LSM: *Where did your love of making comics take you as a teenager?*

DP: Writing comics led to a job at my high school newspaper, which led to an interest in writing. I got all fired up about composing op-ed pieces that were often critical of school policy, and about the way that religion seemed to be constantly favored over alternative ways of thinking (including science and sometimes even common sense). Of course, this got me into lots of trouble at my very strict, Fundamentalist Christian school. Although none of my pieces ever got past the principal's desk, and he did his utmost to discourage my writing and criticize my abilities, a spark had been lit and it stayed lit.

My interest in comics (and other "garbage" reading) also led to an interest in more complex and sophisticated works, including the poetry of E. E. Cummings and the stories and essays of Mark Twain and Henry David Thoreau. I don't think I would ever have made it through a chapter of my favorite book, *Walden*, if I had not first devoured decades' worth of *Mad* magazine and Charlie Brown comics.

LSM: *What do you think about the novelist John Updike's comment that*

the bond between the author of a good children's book and his or her readers is "conspiratorial" in nature?

DP: I agree. Personally, whenever I got the feeling that a book was made just for ME—not for Mom or Dad, *certainly not for Grandma*—it was hard not to feel a bond. I grew up on stories that were proper, straight-laced, adult-approved, Dick and Jane tales of purity and high morality. Those stories were boring to me. It was so refreshing to come across a copy of Thomas Rockwell's *How to Eat Fried Worms* at my local library. That book was for ME.

LSM: *What have you learned about the people who want to ban books? In your experience, do they usually have the same reasons?*

DP: The reasons always surprise me. Once I got into a conversation with someone who told me she enjoyed my picture books, but she did *not* like those Captain Underpants books. She didn't understand why I found it necessary to write about a little boy who flew around in his underwear. I replied, "He's not a little boy. He's a middle-aged man." It soon became clear that this person was complaining about a book she hadn't even bothered to read. She'd just looked at the cover. One of the themes of the Captain Underpants series is to be careful not to judge a book by its cover. But of course it's hard to get that message if you don't read the books.

I've heard a lot of interesting things about Captain Underpants over the years. I've heard that the series is nothing but a bunch of fart jokes, though by my count, there are only about five or six fart jokes spread across twelve books. That's a half a fart per book! Where are all the rest of these farts coming from?

I recently discovered that some people think that I'm a brutish, left-wing liberal nutcase because I gently poked fun at Fox News once. Did they not read *six pages later* where I *also* made fun of the left-leaning *Huffington Post*? I tried to be fair and balanced, but you might miss that if you don't read the books.

I think it's the same thing with comic books and the way they're perceived, due in no small part to Fredric Wertham's *Seduction of the Innocent*, which was an anti–comic book tirade, filled with mostly made-up "facts" and lots of sensationalism that scared the public and gave comic books a bad (and dangerous) reputation. Nobody (myself included) has actually read that book, but if you have any kind of negative associations about comic books, you've been affected by it. Somewhere along the line, somebody wrote about the book's message, and that message got spread. And even though the book's findings have since been debunked, it doesn't matter. The message got out there: "Comic books are dangerous! NO MORE COMICS FOR TIMMY!" Ignorance is contagious.

LSM: *Have your books been challenged or banned in other countries?*
DP: No. The people in every other country I've been to think it's hilarious that the books get banned in the US. They make fun of us for that.

LSM: *What actually happens when one of your books is challenged?*
DP: I have tried to stay out of it for the most part, so I don't usually hear about the challenges until they're all over and done with. I know

that *lots* of people have stood up for my books, because they have told me so.

I haven't gotten any threats or attempts at intimidation beyond the usual name-calling you might expect when one of the boys you've been writing about for twenty years [Harold from Captain Underpants] grows up to be a happily married gay man.

LSM: *Mark Twain, whose* Adventures of Huckleberry Finn *was banned at libraries in his lifetime and afterward, famously crowed that having that happen to a book was good for sales. Has that been your experience?*

DP: Book banning may be good for adult authors, but it hasn't helped my sales at all. I think it's because kids don't usually buy their own books with their own money. They depend on their parents to buy the books, and let's face it: parents are busy. Not all parents have the time or desire to read every book and decide for themselves whether the book is appropriate or not, so if they discover that a children's book has been banned, they might skip that book and buy something different—just to be on the safe side.

LSM: *Do you feel that the divides in people's beliefs that lead to book banning are unbridgeable?*

DP: I'm afraid I do. It's not too surprising, either, especially when you consider how subjective humor is. I mean, you could take two people with similar education, similar IQs, and similar socio-economic backgrounds and ask them about the Three Stooges, and you might get two completely different reactions. One person might say the Three Stooges were comic geniuses, and the other might say they were stupid, violent, and offensive. That's how it goes with humor. You'll never convince someone to think that something is funny when they don't, and vice versa. I feel like I've been very fortunate in this respect. Most people who have read my books have really enjoyed them. The love far outweighs the hate, and that's what I prefer to focus on.

LSM: *Would you talk about your writing and drawing process?*

DP: I think my dyslexia and ADHD have turned out to be a blessing for me as a writer. Having ADHD has made me very aware of the pacing of a story. My hyperactive brain gets sidetracked easily, so I'm very interested in pushing my stories forward on every page. I never want my readers to feel like there's a dull moment—it's important to me that they keep turning those pages to find out what will happen next.

My dyslexia has also been beneficial to my writing process. It's made me aware that there are all kinds of readers out there, and I believe that the things that help me to stay engaged and focused can help readers of all ability levels. For example, I get overwhelmed sometimes when I come across large blocks of text. So I tend to gravitate toward books that have lots of illustrations to break up the chunks, especially if there is an interesting or playful interaction between the pictures and the words. Because of this, graphic novels are something I am most drawn to.

My dyslexia played a large role in the creation of the Captain Underpants series, especially in how the books were designed.

There is always at least one picture on every page, which breaks up the large blocks of text. Each book also contains comic-book chapters, as well as special "Flip-O-Rama" chapters, where simple animation can be achieved by flipping a single page back and forth. These elements give readers a break from all the text and help make the experience of reading feel more like playing than doing homework.

LSM: *When making choices about the jokes and situations you put into a story, have you ever thought that something might be going "too far"? Do you think about what some people refer to as "appropriateness" in a children's book?*

DP: I don't think about imposing limits on myself as a storyteller. I just try to be honest and treat my readers with the respect they deserve. Unfortunately, some people have criticized me for writing a short scene in one of the Captain Underpants books [*Captain Underpants and the Sensational Saga of Sir Stinks-a-Lot*] that includes a family with two dads. There was no sex or kissing or romance in the scene. It was just a few pages that showed two healthy, loving families. One of the families had straight parents, and one had gay parents. That was it. I was accused of being a pervert and of unimaginable depravity. What I found perplexing was that many of these critics complained that they now had to explain to their six-year-old kids that gay people exist and sometimes gay people can get married and have kids. I wasn't sure how to respond to these angry folks. If the reality you've constructed for yourself and your family can be shattered by a children's book, maybe children's books aren't the problem.

LSM: *Would you talk more about your decision to identify Harold as gay?*

DP: Like I said earlier, Harold started out as the shy, awkward, introverted side of my personality. Over the years, however, he became his own person. I think it was around book three in the Captain Underpants series when I began to suspect that Harold was gay, but I never thought it would come up. The books aren't about identity, and I never wanted to write about anything besides George and Harold's friendship.

I wanted the adult versions of George and Harold to both have loving spouses and families. So, when it came time to write those actual pages, it seemed inauthentic to write about Harold and his wife. One of the themes of the Captain Underpants series is "be true to yourself." So I wrote about Harold and his husband, and it was no big deal. Like George and his wife and kids, Harold and his husband and kids are a perfectly normal, loving family. Neither family is particularly special or interesting or noteworthy.

LSM: *The great popularity of your books has given you the chance not only to entertain kids but also to express yourself on some serious themes of importance to them. Do you think of doing the latter as a kind of responsibility?*

DP: I don't really think of it as a responsibility. I've never said, "Next I'm going to write a book about cultural inequality." If a complex theme comes up organically, however, I try to handle it honestly. My newest book was born while I was reading John Steinbeck's *East of Eden*, and I found myself thinking about the nature of our character as human beings. Are we products of our DNA, or of our environment, or a combination of both? In researching the book, I spoke with a prominent child psychiatrist who firmly believed that we are neither. He was 100 percent convinced that we are who we are, and that our families and our environment play absolutely no part in who we are. *Dog Man and Cat Kid* was written around that idea. I admit it's a complex theme, but it came about naturally because I was reading Steinbeck. It was organic. I don't want to shy away from sophisticated themes just because some of my readers are under five years old.

LSM: *In* Captain Underpants and the Preposterous Plight of the Purple Potty People, *you found a humorous way to point up the foolishness of people who ban books like* Heather Has Two Mommies *(*Mommy Has Two Heathers *in your tongue-in-cheek version).*

DP: I don't think book banners need my help to make them look foolish.

JUSTIN RICHARDSON
Born 1963, New York, New York

PETER PARNELL
Born 1953, New York, New York

As a psychiatrist, educator, and author, Justin Richardson has played a pivotal role in training parents, medical professionals, teachers, and others about the importance of providing young people with information and guidance concerning their sexual development and orientation. As a gay man working within a discipline that once considered homosexuality a disease, Richardson has long been acutely aware of the misconceptions and fears that have inhibited open, fact-based discussions of these matters, especially where children and teens were concerned. Working for productive change in this area became a major focus of his professional practice, first as a faculty member at Columbia University and then also as a consultant to grade-school communities nationally. Somewhat to his surprise, a project begun more or less on impulse—a picture book coauthored with his husband, Peter Parnell— turned out to be among the most effective steps he could possibly have taken toward realizing his goal of creating a more open atmosphere for conversations about gender, identity, and family.

Peter Parnell had not been planning to write a children's book, either, when Richardson happened on to the *New York Times* article that triggered the idea for *And Tango Makes Three*. An accomplished playwright and producer, Parnell had had his first major off-Broadway production while still in his twenties, when Joseph Papp's cutting-edge Public Theater staged his romantic comedy *Sorrows of Stephen*. He went on to build a long-term association with another of the city's most innovative theater companies, Playwrights Horizons, and to see his work regularly performed on and off Broadway and across the United States. As television drama entered a new golden age in the late 1990s, Parnell expanded his own horizons as a producer for *The Guardian* and *The West*

Wing and—not to be pigeonholed—as a script writer for *Little Bear*, the animated television show based on a series of classic children's books written by Else Holmelund Minarik and illustrated by Maurice Sendak. His discussions with Sendak served Parnell well years later when he and Richardson suddenly found themselves knee-deep in penguin research and the mysteries of picture-book creation.

The *Times* article that caught their attention told the story of two male penguins living in the Central Park Zoo who had bonded as a couple. After they tried quixotically to hatch out a rock together, a resourceful zookeeper gave the pair a real penguin egg to sit on. The experiment worked, and in due time a penguin chick was born. The outsize success and controversy that followed the publication of *And Tango Makes Three* later prompted the *Times* to revisit the Central Park Zoo story in an interview with the authors who had made the penguins' improbable quest famous among children. Richardson explained that one reason the initial article had so captivated them was that he and Parnell had been trying at the time to have a child of their own by the process of in vitro fertilization with a surrogate mother: "When we heard about the penguins going and getting a rock, we completely understood that urge to have a child." In what the *Times* called "yet another example of life imitating art, or at least humans imitating animals," Richardson and Parnell's daughter was born in February of 2009.

It was fascinating to hear both a theater person's and a therapist's unique perspectives when Parnell and Richardson took part in the panel discussion I moderated at Bank Street College's 2016 conference on the censorship of books for young readers. We met more recently to record this conversation in their New York apartment.

LEONARD S. MARCUS: *Neither of you set out to be a children's book writer. How did it happen that together you wrote one of the most frequently challenged children's books of recent times?*

JUSTIN RICHARDSON: I moved to New York in 1994 after completing my psychiatry residency at Harvard Medical School and started the Columbia University Center for Gay and Lesbian Mental Health. This was in Columbia's Department of Psychiatry, where there were many gay psychiatrists but nobody had ever felt supported enough to create a service for gay patients. There was a long history of stigmatization and mistreatment of gay patients by psychiatrists, so I felt that it was really needed.

Columbia had already established an HIV research center, and a few months after I arrived, the staff there got a call from a consortium of the three most prestigious private girls' schools in Manhattan. The caller said they wanted to begin talking with their students about HIV and asked if some experts from Columbia could come and meet with the heads of their schools. The HIV researchers said yes and asked me to join them. On the way to the meeting, one of them said, "You know, we don't think they need to talk to the girls about HIV so much as they need to talk to them about sexual orientation. Nobody at these schools is having that conversation." So we went into our meeting, and that is what we told them. We said, "Some of your girls are growing up to be lesbian. Some of their teachers are lesbian. None of your teachers are out. Nobody's talking about this. Why isn't that happening, and how can we help you make that happen?"

LSM: *How did they react?*

JR: It was an electrifying meeting, and the result was that these three schools invited me to speak to the teachers, and then to the students, and then to the parents. I began speaking at other schools in New York and then all up and down the East Coast and on the West Coast. We had data that clearly showed that boys in particular who were aware that they were gay were more likely to make a suicide attempt than those who weren't, and that there was a specific risk period, which was the period after they realized that they were gay but before they told anybody. So there was a public health reason to try to reach these kids and give them an opportunity to talk. One of the first girls' schools I had spoken at hosted a wonderful traveling exhibit called Love Makes a Family, with photographic portraits of gay and lesbian families. It caused a small uproar, and the school invited me back to talk to the parents of students in the lower grades about their feelings about the exhibit and how, from an expert perspective, we could help them understand how this was not actually harmful to the kids. Some of the parents were very supportive, but the ones who showed up at the meeting tended to be the ones who were upset. They felt that the exhibition was "inappropriate," that the photographs were "provocative."

LSM: *What worried them the most?*

JR: I think many of them were concerned—and came close to voicing this—that if you broach the topic of sexual orientation with your child, it will make your child more likely to be gay or lesbian; that there is a certain granting of permission that is implied in simply talking about these issues. I was there to explain that that is not actually how sexual orientation develops in children and adults. Some people found it helpful to hear that.

LSM: *What other sorts of help did they want?*

JR: They asked, "But how can we present this to our children?" "Age-appropriate" was the phrase that came up again and again, even in the families that felt like they wanted to let their child know that there are some families with two dads or two moms, as was start-ing to happen more and more in these schools. They didn't know how to *say* it, and they were afraid that if they said it in the wrong way, they would somehow be shaping their child's sexual develop-ment, or telling them something that would be damaging, because, they felt, you mustn't talk about sexuality at too young an age to kids—nobody knowing what the right age is.

They also wanted to know what picture book they could share with their children to help them find the language for this. I explained that there weren't many books, and that the best-known one was the original *Heather Has Two Mommies*. They asked, "Well, what happens in that book?" I said, "It's the story of two women who are trying to conceive a child. They go to their doctor, and it's explained that there's a process of artificial insemination." When I said those last two words, the gasps that came from the audience were really pronounced! And the shaking of heads. "No, we can't. We could never share *that* with our children." It was clear that there was a group who were fine with this and a group who were never going to be fine. But there was also this middle group, who wanted to talk about it but didn't know how. For them, the question was, how are we going to do it?

That was the kind of fertile ground into which the *New York Times* article "Love That Dare Not Squeak Its Name" dropped in February of 2004. Peter and I were sitting in the kitchen, reading the paper, and I said to him, "You have to hear this." There was something about the experience of reading the story aloud and about the way it was written that made us think, *This sounds like a children's book.* We were very excited, and we thought that it was so obviously a picture-book story that everybody was going to have the same idea. So I said, "Let's write it today!"

PETER PARNELL: I was the naysayer. As a theater person, I thought at first of the enormousness of the work involved in getting a project done. It wasn't until we started to put the story together in our own way that I realized we had something. We wrote the first draft very quickly and sharpened it on successive weekends. Justin had already published a parenting book, so we sent an early draft to his agent.

JR: I think I saw the potential first because I had been in front of so many parents, trying to help them find ways of talking about this. I thought, *This is the answer!* Parents reading a story about the penguins wouldn't have to worry that they were talking about sex.

I would always tell the parents, "You're really talking about family. Sometimes a woman falls in love with a woman. Sometimes a man falls in love with a man. When they get together, they form a partnership and can raise a child."

The fact that it was a story about penguins seemed like such a magical solution. For one thing, penguins don't have visible genitals! For another, male and female penguins look exactly the same, so you don't gender them in your mind. A different pair of animals might not have gone over so well. A few years after *Tango* was published, there was a news report about two male vultures who had paired in the Tel Aviv Zoo. A picture book about them might not have had quite the same reach! So the penguin story just seemed like such a perfect solution that it had to be done—and done quickly.

LSM: *How did you divide the work?*

JR: Now the fun began. Our agent's initial comment was that the tone was a little bit off, that it fell somewhere between being fanciful and being just about the facts. So Peter and I sat down and each wrote a new version. I wrote a just-the-facts version, and Peter wrote one in which the penguins were essentially two gay men— one of whom was Nathan Lane!—both wearing tuxedos and going to the opera. It was a very fun, silly version. That really helped us later, because, although we ended up going with the just-the-facts approach, we found bits of personification had sneaked into it, and this helped us identify and remove them. We had decided it was important to keep it as simple and true to what actually happened as possible. That decision, of course, would later serve us well when the book was challenged.

PP: Although writing a picture book was completely new to us, we had both grown up loving picture books, and I had worked a bit in the theater with Maurice Sendak, who was a good friend, and had learned from him about the relationship of words and pictures and the importance of paring down words. We knew we wanted the text to be as spare as possible. That took a lot of work.

LSM: *What were some of your favorite childhood picture books?*

PP: For me it was *Madeline* because the pictures were so gorgeous.

JR: And for me, *The Story of Ferdinand* was the single most important book, because I was a gay boy who didn't like to roughhouse and fight. Ferdinand preferred to sit and smell the flowers, and so did I. Aside from the fact that it's beautifully written and illustrated, that book reached into my household with a message that neither of my parents could give me. It showed me the power of a book to profoundly shape a child's sense of self.

We both also grew up with *The Little Engine That Could*, the paradigmatic story of a plucky little character who thinks he can't do the thing he really, really wants to do, but he tries and tries and tries, anyway—and then succeeds. We both loved that story, and it was clear to us that that was the penguins Roy and Silo's story, too.

LSM: *Did you know what the core of your story was from the start, or did your understanding of it change from draft to draft?*

PP: As we retold the story to ourselves and to friends, we found that we felt an especially strong emotional connection with Roy and Silo at the moment in which they try to hatch a rock. Our friends reacted in the same way as we did—and would cry. So we knew that was one of the story's most emotionally resonant moments. It's presented on a right-hand page, so that you have to turn the page to find out if that is the end for Roy and Silo or if they continue trying.

LSM: *Were you in touch with Henry Cole, the illustrator, during the time that the book was a work in progress?*

PP: We were lucky to have a say in the selection of the illustrator and only wanted one who would be willing to be collaborative. When our editor suggested Henry Cole, Henry wrote a letter saying why he wanted to illustrate our book.

JR: Then Henry came to New York, went to the zoo with us, and made drawings to show what the style of the illustrations might be like. We loved his approach. He knew immediately what the level of realism versus fancifulness should be. There could be a little hint of a smile on the beak of a penguin, but it wasn't going to become silly or comically broad. We worked closely with him at every stage and later with Dan Potash, our wonderful art director, too.

LSM: *Did you reach out to other people for help with research?*

PP: We contacted the writer of the *Times* story, Dinitia Smith, and Rob Gramzay, keeper of the penguin enclosure at the Central Park Zoo, to make sure that we got our facts right. Rob took us behind the scenes and answered many questions. For example, we were concerned about the sameness of the background in the illustrations set in the enclosure, where the wall is painted a uniform solid blue. Rob told us that because the penguins needed to have a sense of the time of day, at sunset he changed the lighting so that the background became a dark orange color. You see that at the end of the book.

JR: There was one line in the final draft that Rob told us he was unhappy with. We wrote, "Rob Gramzay noticed the two penguins and thought to himself, *They must be in love.*" Rob said in response, "You know, I wouldn't use the word 'love' for penguins. I think about 'pair-bonding,' and it's not the same." We appreciated that, but we felt it was important to have that statement in the book. Since we weren't anthropomorphizing the penguins, and since they weren't speaking for themselves, and because the book starts by saying these two male penguins were 'a little bit different . . . they did everything together,' we felt that we had to make it clear that this was different from two boys simply playing together all the time. Children, when they get to choose, typically play in same-sex pairs from first grade to fifth grade, so that's what children understand. We needed to make it clear that this was more like Mommy and Daddy, or Mommy and Mommy, or Daddy and Daddy.

PP: This goes to the heart of the controversy that has surrounded the book. On one level, it's a true story about two penguins. On another level, the book is about something having to do with human experience. In a play, there is usually a metaphor at work under the surface that at some point the audience recognizes, if only subconsciously. It's at that moment that the audience realizes, *Ah, that's the reason this play exists!*

LSM: *So the moment when you say the penguins are in love is the moment when the penguin world and the human world converge.*

JR: That's right, and the human world steps a little bit in front of the other world just there. Even before the book was ever formally challenged, there were a number of news articles that addressed this particular issue. Some writers questioned whether *Tango* was meant as an argument in favor of same-sex parenting. Others simply stated that that was the case.

LSM: *What were some of the other early reactions to the book?*

JR: *Tango* was published at almost the same time that the wildly popular movie *The March of the Penguins* was being shown in theaters. Some people assumed it was the movie version of our book! A few conservative writers pointed to the movie as a demonstration of the theory of intelligent design and the biological basis for monogamy. But when that argument made the rounds of the op-ed pages, other critics, citing *Tango*, turned the argument on its head. "If you think this is an example that should be followed, then what about the two penguins in the Central Park Zoo?" they said. "There's a popular children's book that shows penguins are gay! Are you suggesting that humans should be gay, too?"

Not long after our book was published, the *Chicago Tribune* reported that a female penguin named Scrappy had been introduced into the penguin enclosure at the Central Park Zoo, and that after six years as a couple, Roy and Silo had broken up, and Silo had gone off with Scrappy. On hearing about this, conservatives rose up in triumph: "You see, even penguins can't sustain gay relationships!" When the *Times* interviewed us about this, I said, "Look. The book is no more an argument in favor of same-sex parenting than it is a call to children to sleep on rocks and swallow their fish whole. There are many good reasons to support gay families. The fact that birds do it is not one of them. *Tango* is not a political argument; it's a tool for talking about same-sex families, and it's a spreading of the word about the reality of these families, and not just in birds." It's both a true story about penguins and an opportunity to talk about human families, and the fact that some people experience it as subversive is because it is packaged as "A" but has the impact of "B."

LSM: *What was the first formal challenge to* Tango?

JR: The first was at the Rolling Hills, Missouri, public library. Two parents complained about the book, which the library had initially shelved in new children's fiction, a section popular with browsers. They argued that children would take the book home, and then the parents would read it and discover that it was not "in keeping with their values." Following the complaints, the library director, Barbara Read, moved *Tango* to the nonfiction section, which she rationalized by saying it was a true story, but which, as she explained to the press, she had really done because kids didn't browse there. That way, she was quoted in a local newspaper as saying, no family would be "blindsided" by the book. The article was picked up by the Associated Press, and it went literally around the world. On Comedy Central's *Colbert Report*, Stephen Colbert held up a copy of *Tango* and called it "the number two threat to the American way of life." Number one, he said, was "people who are not blond." Then, in mock disgust, he flung the book across the studio.

Sometime later, we were dismayed to see that the American Library Association's newsletter *American Libraries* had chosen to defend the Missouri library's handling of the situation. The article ended with a quote from Barbara Read that was meant to sum up why the library's actions had been reasonable. "'The bottom line,' Read said, 'is that *Tango* will remain accessible so the book can say to kids in non-nuclear families that they—the kids—are okay regardless of how we feel about their parents' life choices.'" My head exploded when I read that. We responded with a letter to the magazine's editor, to the president of the ALA, and to Judith Krug, who headed the ALA's Office for Intellectual Freedom and was a fantastic champion of *Tango* from the moment we met her.

This is how we ended our letter:

Perhaps we don't need to explain what in particular we found troubling in this quote. But for the sake of clarity we will say that we were disturbed by the heteronormative naming of families with two mothers or two fathers as 'non-nuclear families'; the care with which Ms. Read points out that it is the children of those families, not the families themselves, that are okay; the assumption that the 'we' being addressed are all heterosexual; the assumption that the way we feel about gay adults is negative; and the out-dated and erroneous reference to homosexual orientation as a 'life choice.' Ms. Read is of course entitled to hold all of these opinions, but we are distressed that none of them were challenged by the staff of *American Libraries* if indeed they were noticed.

So that was our first challenge. We were excited to see our book being written about all over the world. But we were angry that the American Library Association didn't get it. That was the last time the ALA didn't get it, though, because Judy Krug quickly swung into action and turned the ALA into a very powerful advocate for *Tango*.

PP: Along with the ALA, when challenges arose, the American Civil Liberties Union and the children's division of the writers group PEN made sure that librarians, school boards, school superintendents, and parents around the country knew when and how they were violating the First Amendment.

JR: We had to think about our own role in these challenges. We came to feel that it was important that they be dealt with locally, by the folks who had children in those schools or who patronized those libraries, or by the local gay organizations, or by the local chapter of the ACLU. It seemed more meaningful for a challenge to be resolved by them than for two guys to swoop in from Greenwich Village and announce, "We're here to protect our book." We felt that *Tango* now has a life of its own, that it had its defenders and its detractors, and that their disagreements were best played out community by community.

PP: As a result of our friendship with Judy Krug, we were invited
to speak at the American Library Association's annual conference. From the librarians we met there, we came to understand
better what they were up against as they defended our book and
others. During Banned Books Week, we read *Tango* alongside Judy
Blume, Robie Harris, and other writers on the Top Ten list and
got to know them. We were getting a crash course in intellectual
freedom.

JR: We also learned about self-censorship among librarians. Once a
public-school librarian orders a book and it's in the school library,
that book is protected by the United States Constitution. It's not
leaving the school. What *isn't* protected is the moment, earlier in
the process, when the librarian decides, *Should I order this book or
not?* At that moment, the librarian may be thinking, *How secure
am I in my position? Will my principal stand up for me? What
other books have parents and the school board complained about
in the past?* It's true that parents' complaints about a particular
book usually don't get that book taken out of the library. But they
probably do prevent other similar books from being purchased.

LSM: *How would you sum up the reasons that some people have objected
to* Tango?

JR: There's a diverse set of reasons. First, there's the fear we've already
spoken about that if a child finds out about homosexuality,
he or she will be more likely to be gay, and that would be bad.
So, for some parents, that means concealing knowledge about

homosexuality from their children. Sexual education in this country has been stuck with this point of view forever. Abstinence-only education, for example, is the only form of education I can think of that is based on the premise that withholding knowledge is what's helpful for a child. It obviously makes no sense. But that's the fear.

There is also a small minority of people who object to *Tango* because they fear that children will equate the love that the story is about with sex, which is simply not how young children think. Children respond to the book as a story about family and as a story about trying to get something you want and finally getting it.

PP: They delight in the scene when the egg hatches. When we read *Tango* in schools, the children cheer every time that happens.

JR: They're not thinking about gay sex. But some parents are, and they don't understand that their children's minds are different from theirs.

SONYA SONES
Born 1952, Boston, Massachusetts

Sonya Sones identifies herself as "a card-carrying member of the dangerous authors' club since 2004." That is the year her verse novel for teens, *What My Mother Doesn't Know*, made its first appearance on the American Library Association's annual list of Top Ten Most Challenged Books. Sones chose to regard this and several subsequent ALA list callouts as a badge of honor—and as an opportunity to speak out in defense of freedom of expression. Writing in the *Los Angeles Review of Books*, she explained: "I decided not to let the foolish accusations of self-righteous people stifle the voices of my characters."

Sones came to writing books for teens along a zigzag path that started in animation and led her past stints as a documentary filmmaker, television editor, and, briefly, a children's clothing designer. Poetry at first looked to be one more outlet for her natural gifts for impish clowning and spot-on satire. Then one day, she surprised herself by writing a different, more serious kind of poem that revealed to her an amazing truth: the power of poetry to transform painful remembered words into words that heal. It was one of those earthshaking moments of self-discovery when a young, unformed writer suddenly finds her voice—for Sones, a vulnerable yet defiant first-person voice for channeling the roller-coaster heartbreaks and raptures of being a teenager. Along the way, she also became a superb portrait photographer.

She is an avid collector of comments about censorship by fellow authors. George Bernard Shaw, Kurt Vonnegut Jr., Oscar Wilde, and Mark Twain all had memorable things to say on the subject. Among her favorites is playwright and journalist Clare Boothe Luce's remark about our democratic right to read, write, and think what we wish: "Censorship," said Luce, "like charity, should begin at home; but unlike charity, it should end there."

Sones and I first met at a California writers conference. During the twenty-one years I was *Parenting* magazine's book reviewer, I was always on the lookout for her latest novel in verse. Along the way, she and I also became friends. She was at home in Los Angeles when we recorded this conversation by phone.

———

LEONARD S. MARCUS: *You grew up in New England, where puritanism took hold in America and "banned in Boston" first became a popular catchphrase more than a century ago. Have you been banned in Boston, too?*

SONYA SONES: No, but I've been banned in Bakersfield, not far from my home here in California. I'm very proud of that. Banned in Bakersfield! I love that alliteration. I'm thinking of putting it on my tombstone.

LSM: *Ha! Were you always a rebel, even as a child?*

SS: I was too much of a scaredy-cat to be a rebel. I was more the sensitive-artist type. My favorite thing to do was to go up to our attic and draw pictures of dinosaurs.

I was the youngest of three sisters in a middle-class family. My father sold frozen food, and my mother was his accountant. When I was in tenth grade, my parents changed careers and began selling antiques. This made me very happy, because it meant they would go away almost every weekend to sell their wares at flea markets. And, of course, I loved having the house all to myself!

LSM: *Did you enjoy school?*

SS: Yes, and I especially loved art and writing, even when I was in elementary school. One great memory from that time stands out. We moved in the middle of my fourth-grade year, and I had to switch to a different school. My new teacher asked us to write stories in class. I got so into my story that at the end of the period, I didn't want to stop. Although I hadn't said anything, the teacher somehow understood how inspired I felt and told me I could keep writing until I had finished. I felt so respected and acknowledged as a creative person in that moment. It changed me!

LSM: *In your National Book Festival talk in Washington, DC, you spoke about lying as an essential skill for teenagers.*

SS: Lying was a big part of my teenage life because my overprotective mother basically didn't want me to do any of the things that I felt were essential for my survival. She didn't even want me to go to the free afternoon rock concerts on the Boston Common. I loved taking photographs at those concerts and had lots of important experiences at them. Once, when I was sixteen, I came upon a group that had formed a circle around a woman who was preaching deliriously about Jesus. The woman clearly was mentally ill. But the people in the mob were taking turns shouting out insulting jokes about her as everyone else laughed and cheered. Because my sister Diane had a mental illness, I've always felt protective of people like that woman. So, although I was scared to death, I forced myself to speak up in defense of her, and the mob dispersed. At that point in my life, I'd been struggling with my self-esteem. But finding the courage to take action helped me feel better about myself. It was because of experiences like that one that I felt I *had* to go to those concerts. So I'd lie to my mother, telling her I was going to a friend's house.

LSM: *It's ironic that just as teenagers are coming to terms with morality for themselves, lying can sometimes be the best option.*

SS: Sometimes it feels like the *only* option. At least, that's how it felt to *me*.

LSM: *You started making animated films before you went to college.*

SS: Yes. I had a rough first year of high school. It seemed as if all my friends had left me behind and I felt utterly alone and miserable. So that summer, my mother looked for something fun for me to do and signed me up at the Newton Creative Arts Center. Not only did I find some new friends there, but I took the animation class and fell in love with the art form. I made an underwater fantasy called *Just a Fishment of My Imagination* and knew that I had found my passion.

So I kept making animated films, and when I graduated from high school, I wanted to continue studying filmmaking. The most famous film schools were in California, but my mother didn't want me to go so far away. So I ended up enrolling at Hampshire College, in Amherst, Massachusetts, just a couple of hours away from home. At Hampshire, I made an animated film called *Dinosaurs Are Done For* to satisfy my science requirement, which got me into documentary filmmaking, too.

Whereas my mother always said, "This movie thing is fine, but you should learn how to type in case you have to become a secretary," my dad would always say to my sisters and me, "You can be anything you want. You can be doctors. You can be lawyers. You can be film directors." This was at a time when people rarely said such things to girls, so it was pretty cool of him to have had that kind of encouraging attitude.

LSM: *You later moved to California after all, where you worked as a film and television editor for several years, but you quit when you had your first child.*

SS: Yes, I was lucky, because my husband, Bennett Tramer, was supporting the family, by working as the head writer of the TV show *Saved by the Bell*. But when my daughter took her naps, I found myself with time on my hands. So I started painting animals on little T-shirts for her to wear, because I didn't want to spend twenty dollars on things that she was going to outgrow in three seconds. When people saw the shirts, they wanted to buy them. And all of a sudden, I had this hand-painted baby clothes company, which rapidly grew out of control. Macy's ordered a thousand outfits! And pretty soon I got tired of coming up with new designs—one more cute little duck, one more adorable little bunny. It wasn't creatively satisfying. I looked around at my life and thought about what to do next. By then I had a son, too, and reading to my kids every night was my absolute favorite part of the day. So I decided I'd try to write books for kids. My first attempt was called *Smitty the Hollywood Kitty*. And, boy, oh, boy, did it suck! It was a bad imitation of Dr. Seuss. But it took me an embarrassingly long time to realize that. And when I finally did, I decided to enroll in a poetry class taught by Myra Cohn Livingston at UCLA. Myra taught me everything I know about writing poetry.

LSM: *Why do you think you gravitated toward poetry instead of prose?*

SS: Well, when I was growing up, hurtful words were often hurled at me. They hurt me so deeply that I think becoming a poet gave me a chance to gain complete control over words—to harness their power in a way that only poetry can. Like Sophie, the narrator of *What My Mother Doesn't Know*, I had a mother who would go down into the basement when she was depressed and come upstairs only to cook dinner for the family. This made me feel terribly guilty as a kid. My mother was probably clinically depressed, though she was never diagnosed. I thought her sadness was my fault—especially since whenever she didn't like my behavior, she'd say things like "You're giving me apoplexy! You're killing me!" I'd think, *Oh, my God, I'm killing my mother!* I was such a sensitive kid, it really got to me.

LSM: *How did you discover that the teen voice is your natural writing voice?*

SS: It happened when I was taking Myra's poetry class. When I first enrolled, I wrote only funny poems. I would read my poems aloud in class, and everyone would laugh at my punch lines. Myra would say, "Oh Sonya, you bring us up from the depths. What would we do without you?" And I loved that role—being the funny one.

Then one day, she gave us an assignment to write a poem using somber dactyl and trochee rhythms. When I sat down to do the homework, a poem about my sister Diane's first nervous breakdown just sort of leaped onto the page. I was astonished, because I hadn't been thinking consciously about her at all. But I guess those somber rhythms must have brought it out of me. I was afraid to share the poem with Myra, because I knew it wasn't going to bring anyone up from the depths. And it felt so personal. I decided I couldn't bear to read it aloud in class, but I handed it in to Myra at the end of the session. The class met only once a week, so I had to wait an eternity to hear what she thought of the poem. I admired her so much, and I really didn't want to disappoint her. I thought, *Oh, my God, what will she say?* I was all in a dither!

At our next session, when she handed our homework back to us, I saw that she had written a note in red ink on my poem. It said: "We have to talk about *this* one." My heart sank. I imagined she was going to tell me to stop writing sad poems and go back to being funny. But instead, she took me aside after class and said, "You know you should write *more* poems about your sister. If you can put yourself through it, you'd be doing a service for anyone with a family member who's throwing the whole rest of the family off-kilter." I really didn't want to think about that painful period in my life, but I wanted to please Myra. So I tried to write at least one poem a week about Diane. Whenever I finished reading one of these poems aloud in class, there would be dead silence. At first I thought it was because my fellow students hated them. But then I realized that these poems were moving them, sometimes to tears. And I was overwhelmed by how connected to them this made me feel.

These poems eventually became my first novel in verse, *Stop Pretending: What Happened When My Big Sister Went Crazy.* And writing them, and sharing them with Myra and my classmates, became a way for me to relive the painful experiences I had gone through, only this time I didn't feel so alone. I felt supported by everyone in the room. And as I continued to delve into that period of my life, I remembered something I had forgotten. After visiting my sister in the hospital, I used to feel so freaked out, so tense and upset. But I found that if I went home and wrote down everything that had happened during our visit, I felt better. I felt emptied out—like all that horrible stuff wasn't churning around inside me anymore. Instead it was on the page.

Because I was thirteen when my sister first broke down, the poems about her were written in that voice. And by then, my daughter was thirteen, too. Being around her and her friends made me remember my own teenage experiences. The planets aligned, and I was able to see clearly what it was like to be a teenager now, and also to remember what it had been like to be a teenager myself. So writing in that voice came very easily to me.

LSM: *It was during your sister's first illness that you started keeping a journal?*

SS: Yes, when I was thirteen, and I saved every one of them. So, when I was working on *Stop Pretending*, I dug my old journals out of a box in my closet and sometimes was even able to pull direct quotes from them for my poems. I kept journals well into my adulthood. Later, when my daughter was turning nineteen, I thought it would be nice for me to share with her what I was like at nineteen. So I found the journal I had kept that year, and I was going to read some excerpts to her. But when I took a look at it, I realized it was nothing but descriptions of sunsets! I was so disappointed.

LSM: *How did you first find out that one of your books had been challenged?*

SS: In 2004, my editor, David Gale, called to tell me that *What My Mother Doesn't Know* had just made the Top Ten Most Challenged Books list of the year. I was stunned. Not only because the book had been out for three years already but also because it had been criticized for "sexual content" and "offensive language." I thought, *Whaaaaat?* There's no sex in the book! There's no cursing! Not even any drinking or drugs! There was nothing in it, as far as I could see, that would make people want to ban it.

LSM: *Then why was it banned? And why do you think it happened when it did?*

SS: Possibly because 2004 is the year it became available in paperback, which meant that a lot more people, including parents, read it and had a chance to be offended!

LSM: *Is* What My Mother Doesn't Know *your most frequently challenged book?*

SS: Yes. I also get an occasional challenge for *What My Girlfriend Doesn't Know* and for *One of Those Hideous Books Where the Mother Dies*. I thought I would get *more* challenges for *One of Those Hideous Books* because of Ruby's father being gay and having a boyfriend. I thought that would upset a lot of people. And probably it did. But at the time it was published, American society was just getting to the point of being more accepting of LGBTQ folks, so most of the objectors may have felt they had to find other ways to complain about the book instead of pointing specifically to the father's sexuality.

LSM: *Do you get drawn into local controversies surrounding your books?*

SS: Yes. Often a librarian at a library or school where a book is being challenged will write me a letter explaining what's going on. When that happens, I leap right in and send them back a letter that directly addresses the reason for the challenge. I've found that the parents who object to my books have usually not read the whole thing. They've read only excerpts. Parents often acknowledge as much in the angry letters they send me, complaining about how disgusting and vulgar my book is. But of course, if you take things out of context, a book can seem "vulgar" when it isn't, really. I'll give you an example. As far as I know, there are only two poems in *What My Mother Doesn't Know* that have prompted people to initiate a challenge. One is a poem in which the narrator, Sophie, enters an online chat room and meets a guy named Chaz who, at first, seems utterly charming and funny. So charming and funny that, after chatting with him a few times, she decides to arrange a meeting. But I wanted Sophie to realize that that would be unwise. So I had to have Chaz say something really gross to cause this revelation. When she asks him what his favorite thing to do is, he replies, "I like to jerk off in libraries." This makes it clear to Sophie that she could have ended up in a very dangerous situation. It was absolutely necessary to have a disturbing line like that, to get this point across. But some people, the ones who haven't read the whole book, read that one phrase and get a totally wrong idea about the story.

The other controversial poem is a very short one called "Ice Capades," in which Sophie presses her breasts against the cold windowpane in her bedroom at night so that she can see the amazing tricks her nipples can do. After I wrote that poem, I showed it to my husband and said, "Oh, God, I can't put this into the book." But he said, "It's a great poem. Kids will relate to it. You absolutely should put it in." Later I was happy I'd followed my husband's advice, because I heard from so many girls who read it and told me that it made them feel much less weird about their own bodies. But I guess the people who challenged the book couldn't handle the word *nipples*. Or maybe they thought it was a sexual poem, even though it really wasn't. Sophie was just looking at her own newly developing body and saying, "Wow, look what it can do!"

LSM: *You have described yourself as having been overprotected by your mother as a child and teen. How would you compare your mother's protective impulse to that of the people who challenge books that they fear might be harmful to young readers?*

SS: The difference is that, when my mother forbade me to go to those rock concerts on the Boston Common, she didn't also attempt to keep everyone else from going. It's true that the people who challenge a book are trying to protect their children, but they are also trying to take that same book away from *everyone* in the community. That's where it all goes really, really wrong. I never mind if a mother says to me, "My daughter was reading your book, and I think it's completely inappropriate for her." I always reply, "Well, you're her mother, and it's certainly within your rights to say that she should wait to read a book like mine until she's older." But it's not within her rights to say that none of her friends and nobody in her school or town can read it, either.

LSM: *We talked before about the power of words to cause harm and pain. How did you feel when you found out your books were being challenged, that some people were saying that your words were harming their children?*

SS: I was getting so much positive feedback from my readers that it didn't hit me very hard. Though *What My Mother Doesn't Know* was published before we had social media, we did have email, and I made the radical decision to publish my email address on the last page of the book, along with an invitation to readers to write to me. As a result, I got tons of emails from kids who had just finished reading the book and were thrilled that they could communicate with me right at that very moment. They said things like "Your book taught me that I shouldn't care so much about what people think" and "There was a guy I liked at school, and he wasn't cute. But I went for him, anyway, after I read your book, and I'm so glad I did." I felt like I was getting the homely guys of the world a date! It was very gratifying. I wrote back to every one of those readers. They'd tell their friends, and then *they* would read the book so that they could get an email from an author, too. It just kind of snowballed. I'm sure sales of the book were helped by the fact that it made the American Library Association Office for Intellectual Freedom's annual Top Ten list of banned books in 2004, 2005, 2010, and 2011. But even before that, it had gained a foothold.

LSM: *Have you ever written back to the adults who challenge the book?*

SS: I often have, even though I know it's probably too late to change the mind of an adult who has decided that it's okay to ban books. I tell them that I know they are doing this because they want to protect their child and that maybe my book *isn't* right for their child. But I suggest that they at least read the whole book before they judge it. One of the reasons I'm delighted when I make that Top Ten list is that when my books are banned, schools invite me to speak to their students during Banned Books Week. This gives me a chance to talk to kids about why they should never allow books to be banned in their communities. And if I'm lucky, I'll have a chance to sway them in the right direction before some misguided adult in their life has a chance to sway them in the wrong one.

LSM: *Has having your work challenged affected your writing? Has it made you more cautious—or more defiant?*

SS: Before the first challenges, when I was still working on *What My Mother Doesn't Know*, I wrote a poem about masturbation. My editor and I talked about it. It was so subtle, not at all graphic in any way. But I still decided to cut it, because we thought it might keep libraries from purchasing the book. I would call that decision self-censorship, done in order to give the book a chance to reach more readers. But there were no other instances of it, and my editor never suggested I delete any other poems. Little did we know that some of the stuff I left in would cause such a ruckus!

R. L. STINE

Born 1943, Columbus, Ohio

Whenever a bored or curious young R. L. Stine character steals into a spooky, web-festooned basement or attic, an eerie encounter is bound to ensue, perhaps one involving a creepy ventriloquist's dummy or a secret stash of Halloween masks. As a nine-year-old growing up near Columbus, Ohio, Stine himself had a very different sort of adventure when, while exploring a cousin's house one day, he found a manual typewriter, fell under its spell, and immediately began pecking out stories on the clattering old machine. The magic of the moment never wore off, and from then on, writing has been a major part of his life.

Stine began his career as an author of humorous stories, not spine-tingling ones. But as luck would have it, a savvy friend who was a children's book editor was looking for a scary preteen book to add to her list and asked him to write one. When *Blind Date* became a surprise bestseller, what was he to do? He said to himself, *Forget the funny stuff. Kids like to be scared!* That success marked the start of what has become a world-wide publishing phenomenon, with total sales of his stand-alone novels and Goosebumps, Fear Street, and other series books now measured in the hundreds of millions, making Stine one of the world's most popular authors of all time.

Stine has somehow always known how scary is too scary for his young, impressionable readers. His characters, too, know—or else quickly learn—how to hold excessive fear at bay rather than simply crawl under the nearest rock in terror. Faced with a hair-raising situation, a Stine character typically improvises a clever plan for wiggling his or her way out of it, or hangs on long enough to realize (along with the reader) that it was all just a false alarm—often a dream. As Stine explained to a *New York Times* reporter, "I work very hard to keep these books from being too real. The real world is much scarier than what I write about."

Ironically, the most frightened responses to Stine's children's books have come from adults. The Goosebumps series ranked fifteenth on the American Library Association's list of most frequently challenged books of the 1990s. A decade later, it returned to the list in the ninety-fourth position. Challengers cited the books' scary content (no surprise there) and sometimes their "satanic or occult themes."

I first became intrigued by the power of R. L. Stine's work when, during a visit to my local library with my then four-year-old son, Jacob, I watched as he spotted a face-out copy of Stine's *Werewolf of Fever Swamp* and locked eyes with the picture of the title character. Impressed by his reaction, I asked Jacob if he wanted me to borrow the book for reading at home later. He made it abundantly clear that he did *not*. For this four-year-old, staring down a werewolf had clearly been enough thrills and chills for one day. His emphatic and balanced response fascinated me, and after that, I became very curious about the author who was said to know more than just about anybody about how far young readers are prepared to go for a good fright.

Oddly enough, Stine and I first met at the United Nations head-quarters in New York, at a program about children's literature in which we were fellow panelists. We recorded this interview over coffee in the cozy study of his art- and collectibles-filled Manhattan apartment.

——————

LEONARD S. MARCUS: *John Updike once said that the relationship between the author of a good children's book and his or her readers is "conspiratorial" in nature. Does that sound about right to you?*

R. L. STINE: I like that statement a lot. Nothing makes me happier than when a parent tells me, "My kid never read before, and the other night I caught him under the covers with a flashlight, reading one of your books at two in the morning." That's conspiratorial, and I love that. A lot of times kids will tell me, "We don't read Goosebumps because we don't have it in school," and I'll say, "They're much better at home. Read them on your own. That's much better than having Goosebumps be schoolwork."

There are lots of parents now who are in their thirties who have saved their own Goosebumps books and given them to their kids. I've been doing this for so long that my readership has become multigenerational. If you were ten years old in the '90s, you are in your thirties now. The *Goosebumps* movie did so well because we had two different audiences: the thirty-five-year-olds coming for nostalgia, and their kids. Very strange! I'm nostalgia to the older ones, and it took me a while to get used to being nostalgia. "You were my childhood," they'll say to me; or "You got me through a tough childhood." That, of course, is very gratifying. I hear things like that all the time. It's a little *too* nice!

LSM: *When did you come up with your apt description of Goosebumps as a "safe scare"?*

RLS: I thought of that for the first interviews I did in the 1990s. People would say, "How far will you go with your scares? What do you think is the limit?" I would always say, "Well, kids have to know that it's going to be a scary, twisty ride, and that it's going to have all kinds of surprises, and that there is going to be a happy ending." That's a safe scare. They're in their room at home, reading, and it's safe.

Once for my other, older series, Fear Street, I wrote a book with an unhappy ending, where the murderer gets off scot-free and the good girl is sent to prison. I did it just for a joke, to entertain myself. But the kids hated it, and they turned on me immediately, and I got letters: "Dear Mr. R. L. Stine, You idiot! You moron! How could you write that?" At every school I visited, someone would raise their hand and ask, "How did you write that book? Why did you do that? Are you going to write a sequel to finish the story?" They couldn't accept it. It *had* to have a happy ending. So I wrote a sequel!

LSM: *Did you see yourself becoming a kind of Pied Piper character, writing stories that kids found tantalizing and that the grown-ups around them did not always want them to have?*

RLS: I never thought of it that way. I knew we weren't doing anything terrible. The whole idea behind Goosebumps was reading motivation—getting kids to read. Everyone was complaining back then in the 1990s that kids weren't reading. So that was the real point of it. There had never been a scary series for seven- to twelve-year-olds, and I think that's one of the reasons we got a lot of criticism in the beginning: it was a first, and people did not know what to think about a book series that was basically designed to scare kids.

LSM: *You seem very aware of the psychology of your readers. Kids of those ages want to test themselves.*

RLS: The psychology of the series is basically this: the kids are always totally normal kids. They're not exceptional in any way. They're facing a huge problem—a monster or a ghost or a zombie—and their parents are useless! The parents are always useless, either because they don't believe their kids or because they're not around. The parents never help. So the psychology of the stories is that you have to use your own wits to defeat whatever the evil thing is. That's it. That's every book. There are no other moral lessons. Nothing!

LSM: *The stories are as much about friendship as they are about being scared.*

RLS: That's true. There's always a boy and a girl and a lot of friends. They're all twelve years old, and they work together, say, to counter a bully. I don't know why, but I love writing bullies. I make sure that somehow the bully always comes into the group by the end.

Interestingly, a lot of kids identify with the monsters. A lot of kids feel out of control sometimes. They feel angry. They feel that they don't belong, that they're different, and they want to rage. They want to tear things apart. That makes the monsters in my books very appealing to kids.

LSM: *Your characters show one another that it's okay to be afraid.*

RLS: They're afraid together, but they're all afraid. There's never one brave one.

LSM: *It seems that imagination is closely related to fear. The bigger the imagination, the bigger the scare you can give yourself.*

RLS: That's good!

LSM: *For instance, in the very first Goosebumps book,* Welcome to Dead House, *Amanda hears mysterious footsteps, then realizes it's just the sound of rain hitting the roof. Later, she sees the other children encircling her and her brother in what feels like a menacing way. But then she decides they aren't really being threatening, that it's just her overactive imagination playing tricks on her again.*

RLS: Well, that's one of my techniques. Kids will imagine things that are much more horrible than what is actually happening to them.

I actually think that *Welcome to Dead House* was too scary. I'd been doing the teen series, Fear Street, which was all about teens and terror. Initially, when the idea for Goosebumps was suggested to me, I didn't want to do it at all, because I thought that kids of seven to twelve might be too young an audience. When I wrote the first Goosebumps book, I didn't yet have down the combination of humor and horror that makes the series work. By the time I wrote the second one, *Stay Out of the Basement*, I had found the humor part. I had started out writing joke books and writing and editing a humor magazine called *Bananas*, so for a long time, humor was all I cared about. With *Stay Out of the Basement*, I found a way to work humor into the Goosebumps books and lessen the scares. That's why whenever things get really intense, I put in something funny.

I don't *really* want to terrify kids. I love the Goosebumps age group, which I think is the best audience a writer could have, because they are enthusiastic about life in a way that they will never be enthusiastic again. After that, kids discover sex, their personalities change, and they have to be cool. But kids of seven to eleven or twelve love authors, want to talk to you, want to buy stuff, and want to show you what they can do. Sometimes they want to tell me scary stories! And they want to be taken seriously.

LSM: *You often show how competent your young characters are.*
RLS: They have to be, with such useless parents!

LSM: *What about you? What were you like, growing up?*

RLS: I was a very shy and very fearful kid. I grew up in a little suburb near Columbus, Ohio, and I used to ride around the neighborhood on my bicycle at night. I always thought that someone or something was lurking in the garage, waiting for me. I would take my bike and just heave it into the garage and run into the house because I was scared.

LSM: *Home is supposed to be the safe place, yet kids have fantasies like the one you just described, which are about the opposite of feeling safe. Is that because the imagination always has to test the limits and edges of things?*

RLS: I think it's just because home is what kids know. They're either at home or they're in school. That's their world. All my books take place in backyards, kitchens, familiar places like that—never in a castle in Middle Europe. Also, kids get their ideas about things culturally. You don't automatically think that a basement is a scary place, but you see cartoons or movies based on that idea when you're a little kid, and then you have the idea, too: *Oh, it's dark and scary down there!*

LSM: *You were the oldest of three children. Did that make you the "responsible one"?*

RLS: My parents weren't great parents, but my mother sort of doted on me. My wife, Jane, says that I was an only child with a brother and a sister. When I was in junior high, I realized that I was the grown-up in the family. I was the adult. My sister was seven years

younger than me, but my brother and I were close. I would take him to school and back every day, and we'd go to see horror movies together every Saturday morning.

LSM: *Did you read comic books?*

RLS: I loved horror comics like *Tales from the Crypt* and *The Vault of Horror*. They had amazing art and gruesome, horrible stories with a funny twist ending. They were very influential for what I do! The writers and artists understood what I think is the closeness of humor and horror. They cause the same visceral reaction. If you sneak up on somebody and go "Boo!" what do they do? First they gasp, and then they laugh. They have both reactions. Or if you go on the roller coaster at an amusement park, what do you hear? You hear people screaming and laughing at the same time.

LSM: *Humor and horror are both about being out of control, aren't they?*

RLS: Yes, that's right. I should add, though, that it is probably because there is something missing in my brain that horror doesn't ever scare me. When I read Stephen King, I never get scared. I go to horror movies. I'm always the one laughing. People tell me, "I read your book, and I had to keep the lights on all night, and I locked all the doors." I've never had that experience! The shark comes up. He eats the girl. I don't know why, but horror makes me laugh.

LSM: *You were very young when you started writing, weren't you?*

RLS: I was in fourth grade when I began writing little joke magazines and comic books, hour after hour at home. I was a weird kid.

LSM: *Was being funny a way to make friends?*

RLS: Yes, because I would take the magazines to school and pass them around. None of my teachers encouraged me. They begged me to stop writing! They'd say, "Bob, please don't bring these magazines in anymore." Finally, when I was a junior in high school, our student newspaper's faculty adviser took me aside and said, "You could write a great humor column. Why don't you do that?" I took her suggestion, and that was the first time I was ever in print.

Growing up, I also had marionettes and did hand-puppet shows, and I had a ventriloquist's dummy. I have written fourteen Goosebumps books about Slappy, a dummy who comes to life, and I still don't get why dummies are so interesting. Of course, other writers have written stories about them before me. There's a *Twilight Zone* television episode about a dummy coming to life, and a British horror film from 1945 called *Dead of Night*, which was probably where I got the idea for Slappy. Slappy is so popular that at Halloween, thousands of kids go out as Slappy now. Last Halloween, I gave a talk in Toronto, and forty kids in the audience were dressed as Slappy. I've sold more red bow ties than anyone in Canada! I killed Slappy off in one of the books, but he is so popular that I had to bring him back.

LSM: *Besides being very popular, the Goosebumps books have often been challenged. When the challenges at schools began, how did you find out about it?*

RLS: My editors and I would hear stories. I don't recall too many of the details, but there was one incident in Minneapolis in 1997 that I do remember clearly. Educators, parents, children, and others met there to discuss Goosebumps at a school district "appropriateness hearing" that was broadcast on C-SPAN. I watched the hearing on television from home. They were trying to decide whether or not to keep Goosebumps in the library, following a complaint from a parent who had said she wanted the books out. One of the speakers who came up to the microphone that day was a father who had brought a stack of my books with him. I could see from the way he was dressed that he was a blue-collar worker, and he introduced himself as a single parent. He explained that he could not read to his young daughter both because he worked such long hours and because he had had so little education. He said that he did not want his daughter to grow up to be like him, that he wanted her to be a reader, and that because she wanted to read the Goosebumps books, he wanted those books to remain available at the school library. I cried when I heard that. It was an amazing moment. The school board voted to keep the books.

There have been a lot of attempts to ban the Goosebumps books but not as many as you would think for a horror series for ten-year-olds. We won a lot of the cases.

LSM: *Did you become directly involved in defending the books?*
RLS: No. Early on, I learned that rule number one is: never defend yourself. I was taught that lesson by a media coach when I was getting ready for an interview on the *Today* show.

My publisher did get involved in responding to the challenges. But the main thing that happened was that we had great support from the start from librarians who had seen so many kids reading my books. Librarians would say to me, "You're keeping us in business. You're keeping us open because kids want to come in and read Goosebumps."

There was a conservative columnist named Diana West who for a while made it her mission to attack Goosebumps. She wrote articles about it. She appeared on television, spoke on panels. It seemed that attacking my books was her full-time job! Her theory was that the tingle of fear that you get from reading a Goosebumps story is exactly the same kind of reaction that you get from pornography. So, according to her, Goosebumps was really pornography for kids.

LSM: *You had a nemesis. Did you ever consider turning her into a character?*

RLS: Ha!

LSM: *I read that you did once write a story about a librarian who devours a child.*

RLS: People ask me, "Do you ever go too far?" Actually, I'm pretty conservative when it comes to horror. In fact, my editors are always pushing me to make my stories scarier. They're telling me, "Hype it up!" I knew early on that there were certain things that set people off—demons, for example—so I never wrote about demons. And I've never written a witch. I'm kind of afraid to do that. But there was this one early Goosebumps book called *The Girl Who Cried Monster*. The title character is in the library stacks one day when she realizes that the librarian is literally a monster. The problem for her is that because she is known to have lied to people in the past, nobody will believe her now. And, yes, in my original manuscript, the girl watches as the librarian eats a kid. That was the one time that my editors said, "No, no, no. Not that. That's going too far." In the final version, I put a big bowl filled with live turtles on the librarian's desk. Every once in a while, he would reach into the bowl, grab one of the little turtles, and pop it in his mouth, which of course was better than having him eat a kid. For one thing, the turtles were crunchier.

LSM: *Were you writing that as a comic scene? A scary one?*
RLS: I thought both.

LSM: *Have the terrible stories we see in the news, for instance the stories about school shootings, changed the atmosphere in which your books are read?*
RLS: It's made me stop writing Fear Street books. It's not a good time to be killing teenagers in fiction. Goosebumps is different, though, because it isn't about real-world problems or situations. They're fantasies.

LSM: *Is it true that* The Haunted Mask *is your favorite Goosebumps story?*
RLS: It's my best Halloween story, and it is the only one of my stories that is based on something that happened in real life. One year at Halloween when our son, Matt, was little, I looked into his room

from the doorway and saw that he was down on the floor trying on a green rubber mask of Frankenstein's monster. I watched as he tried to pull the mask off his face but couldn't. He was tugging and tugging. I should have helped him, right? Instead, I stood there thinking, you know, making mental notes: *Great story idea—a mask that sticks to the kid's face!* I'm very proud of that story.

LSM: *Looking back, do you think that writing scary stories opened something up inside you that you hadn't realized was there?*

RLS: I don't know about that, but before I started writing the scary stuff, I would have a recurring nightmare about being chased. In the dream, I was at home and would run to another room, but the thing that was chasing me, whatever it was, would be in that room, too. It was a really frightening dream. I felt I was being menaced. I had that dream maybe twice a month for years. But as soon as I started writing the scary books, it was gone. I never had the dream again. I guess after that, it all came out at my typewriter.

ANGIE THOMAS
Born 1988, Jackson, Mississippi

Angie Thomas grew up in Jackson, Mississippi, not far from the site of the murder of civil rights leader Medgar Evers, in June of 1963. Angie's mother, Julia, believes she heard the fateful shot. Thirty years later, when five-year-old Angie was nearly caught in the cross fire of a daylight shooting in a neighborhood park, Julia Thomas responded by taking Angie to the local library, hoping to show her child another, better side to life in Jackson. The plan worked well, and the younger Thomas swiftly advanced from avid reader to ardent writer—a writer, at first, of fantasy fiction. Later, a college professor urged her to consider addressing subjects that were closer to home. When Thomas expressed doubts that experiences like her own could have value as material for fiction, he replied, "There are stories there that need to be told and heard, and there are voices there that have been silenced. And if you want to, you can have the opportunity to give those voices a platform through your writing."

The Hate U Give developed from a short story written in response to her teacher's urgings. The title was suggested by a tattoo worn by the rapper and poet Tupac Shakur, whose work had long inspired her. It refers to Tupac's belief in the dire prospects for a society that fails to love its children.

Interest in Thomas's manuscript, which dealt frankly with the circumstances surrounding the fatal shooting of an unarmed Black teenager by a white police officer, was swift and intense. Thirteen publishers vied for the right to publish it, and on the novel's release, in February of 2017, *The Hate U Give* placed number one on the *New York Times* bestseller list for teen fiction. Several awards and a movie deal followed. So, too, did attempts to ban the book. The first well-documented challenge came in November of 2017, in the Katy (Texas) Independent School District, where, in violation of the district's own rules, Thomas's novel was removed from school library shelves while the formal challenge process was still running its course. *The Hate U Give* appeared on the American Library Association's list of Top Ten challenged books in 2017 and again in the following year.

As all of this was happening, Thomas was at work on her next novel, *On the Come Up*, a story about the obstacles faced by an aspiring teen rapper. Initially Thomas had thought about writing her second book— a notoriously difficult hurdle for authors—in a lighter vein. But when the first challenges to *The Hate U Give* blindsided her, she locked on to censorship as a central theme. In *On the Come Up*, sixteen-year-old Brianna battles repeated efforts to distort the meaning of her words as well as attempts to silence her altogether. Days before its release, Thomas told the *New York Times* what her new book meant to her: "I was raised knowing that when hip-hop spoke up, it was always challenged. . . . My mantra is: I want to write the way rappers write."

Thomas and I spoke for the first time for this interview. She was at home in Jackson, Mississippi, when we recorded it by phone on September 3, 2019.

————

LEONARD S. MARCUS: *Early in* On the Come Up, *when Bri is being unfairly criticized at school for being aggressive, her response is to play with the word* aggressive *in her mind and turn it into a rap lyric. She takes a hurtful label and changes it into something that gives her a sense of control, maybe even power. When did you first realize that words can be powerful?*

ANGIE THOMAS: That's a good question! I'd like to say it was third grade, because it was right around then that I realized writing was something I loved to do. At school, I always finished my work ahead of time—I was *that* kid—and one day, while everyone else was finishing up their tests, I took out my little notebook and started writing a story. That's what I liked to do in my free time. When my teacher came up the aisle to make sure that none of us was cheating, she looked over my shoulder, saw what I was doing, and read the story as she stood there. I got scared and thought I was in trouble, and when she asked me what I was doing and

I said, "Nothing," she replied, "Is that a story?" When I admitted, "Yes . . . ," she allowed me to get up in front of the class when everybody was finished and read my story to them. I had ended the story on a cliff-hanger even though I didn't know what that was! And they were, like, "Wait! No! You can't end it there!" It was in that moment, reading the story to them and seeing how attentive they were, and how invested they were in these words I had written down, that I realized words are powerful if you use them in a certain way. That was the moment I became a writer.

LSM: *You have often spoken about the importance of the public library to you then, too.*

AT: The library became my second home. For me, having the library to go to was like having a gigantic key to the rest of the world. I spent so much time reading books at the library that the librarian would say, "You do know that you can take the books home." I would say, "Yes, but I want to read this one *right now*." It's so important for kids to have that opportunity, because so often, depending on factors like lack of transportation and financial means, they are isolated from the world and might never get the chance to go beyond their neighborhood. To know that there is a larger world is extremely important. That is what the library allowed me to know.

LSM: *Is that where you discovered Mildred D. Taylor's* Roll of Thunder, Hear My Cry?

AT: Yes, and I still remember the day the librarian said to me, "I have a book that I think you might like." Before that, I had rarely read a

book about a Black girl and had never read one about a Black girl from Mississippi. Finding that book blew my mind. It's important for kids to know that they can be the main character of a story, that they can be the hero. I remember taking that book home and not wanting to bring it back. That was the first time I got a late fee!

LSM: *Cassie [the protagonist of* Roll of Thunder, Here My Cry*] is defiant and has to face down a lot of prejudice in her day-to-day experience. Was she a model for Starr [in* The Hate U Give*] or Bri?*

AT: One thousand percent. Both of them. I think that every single young Black girl character I will write for the rest of my career will have little bits and pieces of Cassie Logan sprinkled within her. Her strength, her flaws, all of it, because Cassie could be a little bit of a hothead. At the time, I thought that side of her was so cool, but now, as an adult, I'm, like, "Oh, wow!" She was the ultimate heroine. We talk a lot about strong girls in young adult books, and nobody brings her up, and it kind of bothers me, because this was a young woman who faced so much and was so passionate about what she believed in and about her family and about standing up for herself. Bri and Starr both have bits and pieces of her in them. I was also inspired by Cassie's family when I was crafting Starr's family in *The Hate U Give*. I even got Starr's father Maverick's name from *Roll of Thunder*.

LSM: *I read that in college you tried writing fantasy fiction, and I wonder if your experience was anything like that of the Chinese American author Laurence Yep, who said that he started out writing about space aliens because he felt like such an alien himself in white America?*

AT: Oh, yeah. I've been thinking about that a lot. I went toward fantasy because I didn't feel that stories about real people like me would even be published. I was a huge Harry Potter fan, and the reason I loved Harry Potter was that I assumed Hermione was Black. When I saw the movie, I was, like, "Oh." That's nothing against Emma Watson, but it was an "oh" moment for me.

LSM: *Why had you thought that?*

AT: Because I wanted to think it. It was a want thing. Plus, J. K. [Rowling] only described Hermione's hair. She never described her skin tone. And when you tell me about big, curly, unruly hair, that sounds a lot like Black hair. I saw so much of myself in Hermione that I just automatically thought that she must be like me.

LSM: *The power of literature! I like that. When did rap music come into your life?*

AT: Rap music came into my life when books started failing me. That was around my early teenage years, when I wasn't finding a lot of books that I could connect with. I listened to hip-hop music, and that is where I found the stories I needed to hear about the world right around me.

I learned so much about storytelling from hip-hop. I wouldn't be the writer I am without it. I learned to choose my words wisely, to remember that every word has to be *the* word. I learned about being honest and real and authentic with your art and about telling stories even when they make people uncomfortable. Hip-hop was there for me when I needed it, and it also unlocked something inside of me.

LSM: *Is Bri's father, Lawless, a tribute to Tupac Shakur?*

AT: You're the first person to ask that. Absolutely. I would say that both father figures in my novels have a little bit of Tupac in them. For me, as someone who did not have a father active in my life, Tupac was the male figure I learned from. When Tupac talked to Black women through his music, he was talking to me and was telling me the things that I needed a father to tell me. Maverick is like what Tupac probably would have been like if he hadn't been famous and hadn't died young. And in Lawless you see this guy who wanted to do so much but lost his life so early and didn't get a chance to be all that he could have been. What does that kind of loss mean to a young person who sees it happen to someone so close to them? What kind of drive does it give them? That's what Tupac was for me personally. I remember when I was having my twenty-sixth birthday, I thought, *Wow. I've lived longer than Pac did.* I thought about that a lot. And now here I am in my thirties. Pac did so much in such a short time. I think, *What would he be doing now? On Twitter? With the Black Lives Matter movement?* That's why I'm driven to do a lot in the long amount of time that I got.

LSM: *Tell me about the college teacher who encouraged you to write about your own experience.*

AT: His name is Howard Bahr. He's an author who writes Civil War fiction. It often surprises people when I tell them that I was very inspired by an older white guy who writes a lot about Confederate soldiers. They're like, "Really?" But he was the one who made me realize there were stories in my community and stories about people like me that deserved to be told. That was a life-changing moment for me because I had come to assume that stories about Black girls weren't worth being told. This professor told me otherwise. I remember saying to him, "I don't know if people even want to hear this," and him saying back that if even one young lady picks up something that I wrote, sees herself in it, and suddenly feels validated, that's enough. I quickly realized he was right. I'm so grateful to him for showing me that.

LSM: *Starr has to struggle with the two realities she lives in and is forced into a kind of self-censorship much of the time, carefully editing what she says and does. For her, self-censorship is a survival mechanism, isn't it?*

AT: Absolutely, it is a survival mechanism, and for so many kids of color, it is how society is set up—to make them feel that they can't be their authentic selves. They're too *this*, or they're too *that*. Not enough of *this*, or not enough of *that*. Both Starr and Bri are in that struggle. Starr is made to feel that if she doesn't censor herself, she will be considered a threat in her other world. That's really what code-switching is. It's censorship in a world that tells Black people all the time that we are too much or not enough. So we change the way we speak and present ourselves to make other people comfortable, because we are afraid of how they will view us and treat us if we don't. For Starr, it's partly, *I don't want to be seen as ghetto. I don't want to be seen as ignorant.* But it's also, *If they do see me as ghetto and ignorant, how will that change my entire experience in this world?*

LSM: *And with Bri, people are literally trying to put words in her mouth, and she is forced to decide whether or not to allow that.*

AT: Yes, and all the things I went through with *The Hate U Give* being banned in certain school districts were definitely the inspiration for writing about that in *On the Come Up*. I don't think adults think about this, but when you ban a book, what you are essentially doing is telling the kids who see themselves in that book that their story makes you uncomfortable. Their life makes you uncomfortable. They make you uncomfortable. There are kids just like Starr in these schools that are banning the book, and you're saying, I don't want to know more about you. I don't want to know you. That's the message that censorship sends. Thinking about *The Hate U Give*, I asked myself, *What do I want young people to know from it?* You have a voice. Use it. But what are the people who want to ban the book saying? I don't want to hear your voice. I don't like the way you say things. With *On the Come Up*, I wanted to speak to those kids and say, Yes, I told you to speak up and speak out. But I would be doing you a great disservice if I didn't address the fact that so often when you do, people will criticize you for how you say things as opposed to listening to what you're saying. In a lot of ways, the two books are in conversation with each other on the topic of censorship. I hope that the message gets through.

LSM: *Why did you give Starr a white boyfriend? Did you think of it as a hopeful statement about the possibility of young people connecting across racial and class lines?*

AT: I get that question a lot! I gave her a white boyfriend for a couple of reasons. One reason is that I love drama. I thought, *Huh. Starr has this very militant, pro-Black dad. What would burn him up the most? A white boyfriend. What kind of uncomfortable conversations would that lead to?* I wanted to have those conversations. It's not a criticism of Maverick. It's recognizing that his experiences would cause him to see things a certain way, and he would be forced to think about that when it came to his own daughter. In Chris, I wanted to have this young man who is the most privileged person in America. He's young, he's white, he's male, he's straight, he's rich. You cannot get any more privileged than Chris in America. But if he's that privileged, what does it mean that even someone like him can get to a place of listening? A place of awareness? I'm not going to say he's woke, but he's trying to get there. He is getting to a place of understanding and empathy, and that's really what it's all about. I wanted to show that if there's hope for a young man like this, maybe there's hope for some other people.

LSM: *Was Chris a hard character to write about?*

AT: Chris was the hardest character to write. Hailey [a pro–women's rights white school friend who makes racist remarks] was easy because I have dealt with a real Hailey. But Chris was so hard because I didn't know that experience. I wanted to put together this young man who was whole and fully formed and real. It was

so tricky to let him be ignorant at times, because part of me was thinking, he needs to be aware, but at the same time I would think, chances are he would not be *that* aware. He wouldn't know about things beyond his own world. At times, accepting that about him was tough.

LSM: *Do you think the relationship between Starr and Chris might be an unacknowledged reason why* The Hate U Give *has been challenged?*

AT: I wouldn't be surprised if it was. A lot of times the schools will say it's because of the language. But that's not the real reason, considering how many classic novels have curse words in them. I think the real reason the book gets banned is its subject matter, the fact that it's a book about the issues surrounding the Black Lives Matter movement.

LSM: *Did you plan* The Hate U Give *in part with the book's potential critics in mind, for instance, by having Uncle Carlos there to show that there are good cops in Garden Heights as well as violent, racist ones?*

AT: I didn't overthink it. For much of the novel, it was just me coming from my own experience, especially Uncle Carlos, who was based on a relative of mine who was a cop. He would say, "Inside of the uniform, some people see me as a sellout. Outside the uniform, I'm still considered a suspect." I'm thankful that I did include a character like him, because when people try to say the book is anti-cop, I can reply, "No, it's not."

I look at Khalil and the decisions he made before his death. When I was writing him, a part of me wanted to make him a kid who had never done anything wrong. But then I thought, *Well, what if he had? What difference should that make?* I was so used to reading more comments about whether Trayvon Martin was a good kid or a bad kid than about whether or not George Zimmerman should have been charged. So much of the blame is placed on the victim. So, when I was thinking about Khalil, I decided, okay, why make him the perfect kid? Why not make him a kid who has made mistakes? Does that take away from the value of his life? When we're saying Black lives matter, it should mean all Black lives matter, including those of young men like him who have made mistakes. I had Starr question that herself because it was something that I had questioned.

LSM: *In* On the Come Up, *a local reporter, presumably white, writes an article attacking Bri's rap song for inciting violence at her school. But she unwittingly undercuts her argument when she mentions in passing that her own son loves the song. Earlier in the story, the music promoter Supreme says that suburban white kids are the biggest consumers of hip-hop because they love "listening to shit that scares their parents."*

AT: Like video games, hip-hop gets blamed a lot. Nobody thinks about the positive side of hip-hop and what it has done. It has empowered a lot of young people to use their voices, and it has given other young people a window through which to see lives beyond their own. These kids that Supreme is talking about love hip-hop because it's something their parents don't want them to love. What is the underlying message there? It is: Why don't you let me be? Why don't you let me listen to things beyond my own experience, things that make you uncomfortable? This applies to books as well. When you ban a book, it becomes one of the books that kids want the most because you're telling them they shouldn't have it, and they're going to want to know why. The last thing you want is for them to realize that your *why* is weak—and at the end of the day, so many of the whys *are* weak.

LSM: *How did you first find out that* The Hate U Give *was being challenged?*

AT: A librarian from the school district in Katy, Texas, where the first major challenge was made, reached out for advice. Even before that, I had gotten a lot of DMs on Instagram from the students in Katy, who wrote things like "We're so upset. They took your book out of our library. They're banning it, and we want to do something about it. What do we do?" I was brand-new to publishing. This was my first book, and I honestly had not expected the challenges to happen. At first, I was just shell-shocked, and then I felt hurt. And then, all of a sudden, it went from DMs from the students to emails from the librarian to my publisher, and then to the teachers and parents emailing and tweeting, wanting to know what they could do because they weren't happy about what was happening. My publisher told me there were resources and people in place to handle situations like this—the American Library Association and others. But it still felt like a personal attack, especially when I read the articles in which the school district called my book "filth." More so than attacking me, it felt like they were attacking the kids from my neighborhood, and other kids like them, and calling *them* filth. I was angry! I went from hurt to anger and frustration and to feeling misunderstood. That's why all of those emotions ended up going into *On the Come Up*. Bri's feelings are what I felt. I just took their lemon and made a little lemonade.

LSM: *You said before the movie version of* The Hate U Give *was released that perhaps the film would cause some people to read your book with a more open mind. Do you think that happened?*

AT: I do. What the movie did was soften the blow in an interesting way. A lot of times, the people who banned the book hadn't even read it. I could tell that from the things that the librarians told me the school administrators had said, such as, "It's an anti-police book." The film was PG-13, so language and violence weren't going to be issues, and teachers were able to take their students to see it. The conversations about the book became louder as more young people became aware of it because of the movie, and their passion for the story put a lot of administrators in the position of having no choice but to allow their students to read the book. The movie was the best commercial I could ever have asked for!

LSM: The Hate U Give *was also challenged by the Fraternal Order of Police in Charleston County, South Carolina, who in 2018 tried to have it dropped from the Wando High School summer reading list. Did you consider responding directly to that law enforcement organization?*

AT: I did, but then I didn't. My ultimate wish was that they had sat down with the police departments around the country that have

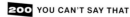

made the book required reading for new recruits. There are several police departments that have done that, or have read it in their book clubs, or sponsored school trips to go see the movie and had discussions with the students afterward—real, open discussions. I wish the members of the Fraternal Order would talk to them, or to the police officers' wives, who love the book. No one is more pro-police than they are, and I have met so many who love the book. They come to my events!

So often people just assume, and then they act on assumptions. At the end of the day, that's what so much of this is about. You make assumptions, and a book may get banned. You make assumptions based on racial bias, and someone dies.

LSM: *You set both* The Hate U Give *and* On the Come Up *in the same place, Garden Heights, and at more or less the same time, but with a different cast of characters. Are you building a world there?*

AT: Garden Heights is very dear to me, and I love showing all the different sides of it. I am working on my third book now, and it's set there as well. It will probably be my last one there, though you never know. If nothing else, I hope I'm showing that even in a neighborhood like that, there are so many stories to be told and so many different lives. If you just look at Starr and Bri: those two girls are so different. They live in the same neighborhood, but they don't even know each other. That was important for me to establish. No, just because they live in the same neighborhood does not mean that they're friends. And more than that, it does not mean that they're alike, or that their experiences are the same.

ACKNOWLEDGMENTS

In April of 2015, I took part in a conference called "Outlawed: The Naked Truth about Censored Literature for Young People," organized by the Arne Nixon Center for the Study of Children's Literature at California State University at Fresno. I left the three-day gathering feeling inspired by the courage and commitment of my fellow presenters, most of them the authors of books that had weathered repeated challenges and bans, and determined to do what I could to help young people appreciate the value of freedom of expression and the importance of safeguarding our First Amendment rights. *You Can't Say That* grew directly out of my experience at that conference and at another one held the following year at the Bank Street College of Education, in New York. My heartfelt thanks to the master planners of those two powerful events: the Arne Nixon Center's then-curator Jennifer Crow and the Bank Street Center for Children's Literature's director Cynthia Weill for their instrumental role in setting me on my path.

You Can't Say That would not have been possible without the all-in cooperation of the thirteen writers I interviewed. I thank them for their time, effort, patience, and passionate involvement. Thanks, too, go to their editors, publicists, and other publishing personnel who coordinated schedules and attended to other necessary details.

I thank Joan Bertin, Steven Shapiro, and Pat R. Scales for generously sharing their knowledge of censorship history and the law. The early support for this project expressed by my late agent, George M. Nicholson, was pivotal to getting it off the ground.

Finally, a tip of my hat to my editor, Hilary Van Dusen; my copyeditors, Pamela Marshall and Hannah Mahoney; and the staff of Candlewick Press for their interest in my work and for their sure-handed guidance at every turn.

SOURCE NOTES

INTRODUCTION

p. xi: "[If] read before the intellect . . . features of crime": Anthony Comstock quoted in Mark I. West, *Children, Culture, and Controversy* (Hamden, CT: Archon, 1988), 13.

p. xi: "trash and . . . for the slums": quoted in Justin Kaplan, *Born to Trouble: One Hundred Years of Huckleberry Finn* (Washington, DC: Library of Congress, 1985), 11.

p. xi: Among the objectors, ironically . . . : "Ban on Twain's 'Finn' Rescinded in Virginia," *New York Times*, April 13, 1982, D27, https://www.nytimes.com/1982/04/13/us /ban-on-twain-s-finn-rescinded-in-virginia.html.

p. xii: "The poet . . . satisfied with them": quoted by Arthur Schlesinger Jr., in *Censorship: 500 Years of Conflict* (New York: New York Public Library, 1984), 7.

p. xii: "The instinct to suppress . . . faith and to fear": ibid.

p. xiv: "diapering . . . tempera paint": quoted in Leonard S. Marcus (ed.), *Dear Genius: The Letters of Ursula Nordstrom* (New York: HarperCollins, 1998), 334.

p. xiv: "representative of several . . . throughout the country": ibid.

p. xiv: "At first the thought . . . obvious suppression": ibid.

p. xiv: "preserv[e] the First Amendment . . . communicating ideas": ibid., 335.

p. xvi: "good decade for writers and readers" and "Almost overnight . . . children's lives": Judy Blume, in "Introduction: A Personal View," Judy Blume (ed.), *Places I Never Meant to Be: Original Stories by Censored Writers* (New York: Simon & Schuster, 1999), 14–15.

p. xix: "Censorship reflects a society's . . . choose for himself": US Supreme Court justice Potter Stewart in his dissenting opinion in *Ginzburg v. United States*, March 22, 1966. *U.S. Reports: Ginzburg v. United States*, 383 U.S. 463, 1965, https://www.loc.gov /item/usrep383463/.

MATT DE LA PEÑA

pp. 1 and 2: "half-Mexican hoop head" and "self-defined nonreaders . . . reading the world": Matt de la Peña, "2016 Newbery Acceptance," *The Horn Book*, June 27, 2016, https://www.hbook.com/?detailStory=2016-newbery-acceptance-by-matt-de-la-pena.

ROBIE H. HARRIS

p. 19: "How can we hold back . . . are afraid?": Robie H. Harris, "Robie Harris on the Banning of Her Books," PEN America, October 15, 2012, https://pen.org/robie-harris-on-the-banning-of-her-books/.

DAVID LEVITHAN

p. 61: "I won the parent lottery . . . friend lottery": Julie Bartel, "One Thing Leads to Another: An Interview with David Levithan," *The Hub* (blog), YALSA, August 29, 2013, http://www.yalsa.ala.org/thehub/2013/08/29/one-thing-leads-to-another-an-interview-with-david-levithan/.

p. 62: "These are exciting . . . publishing" and "We're looking for diversity . . . within that diversity": Nick Duerden, "David Levithan Interview: The US Author on Leading the Way in LGBT Fiction for Young Adults," *The Independent*, March 16, 2015, www.independent.co.uk/arts-entertainment/books/features/david-levithan-interview-the-us-author-on-leading-the-way-in-lgbt-fiction-for-young-adults-10112154.html, March 16, 2015.

MEG MEDINA

p. 75: "I feel like I created . . . approved curriculum": telephone interview with the author, February 15, 2019.

p. 76: "Going from girlhood . . . keep offering girls": Martha Schulman, "Q & A with Meg Medina," *Publishers Weekly*, March 8, 2016, https://www.publishersweekly.com/pw/by-topic/childrens/childrens-authors/article/69601-q-a-with-meg-medina.html.

LESLÉA NEWMAN

p. 89: "Did you ever expect . . . *Has Two Mommies*": Lesléa Newman, "Great Expectations: The Journey of *Heather Has Two Mommies*," *HuffPost*, March 26, 2015, updated December 6, 2017, https://www.huffpost.com/entry/post_9206_b_6929784.

p. 90: "[*Heather*] brought to the forefront . . . to young kids" and "a time when . . . culture wars now": quoted in Leanne Italie, "*Heather Has Two Mommies* Turns 25," *USA Today*, March 16, 2015, https://www.usatoday.com/story/life/books/2015/03/16 /heather-has-two-mommies-turns-25/24858121/.

p. 100: "carry out a program or activity . . . lifestyle alternative": quoted in Elon Green, "Lesléa Newman: So, What Was That Like?," *New Yorker*, April 24, 2014, https://www .newyorker.com/culture/culture-desk/lesla-newman-so-what-was-that-like.

KATHERINE PATERSON

p. 108: "The fact that I call myself . . . God has given me": Katherine Paterson, *The Invisible Child: On Reading and Writing Books for Children* (New York: Dutton, 2001), 158.

p. 109: "Fiction is about everything . . . grand enough": ibid., 159.

DAV PILKEY

pp. 126 and 127: "I guess I really shouldn't . . . banned-books lists" and "My very first . . . very good listener": Dav Pilkey, "What It's Like to Top Banned Book Lists Around the World," *The Guardian*, August 31, 2015, https://www.theguardian.com /childrens-books-site/2015/aug/31/banned-books-captain-underpants-dav-pilkey.

JUSTIN RICHARDSON AND PETER PARNELL

pp. 143 and 144: the *New York Times* article that triggered the idea: Dinitia Smith, "Love That Dare Not Squeak Its Name," *New York Times*, February 7, 2004, B7, https://www.nytimes.com/2004/02/07/arts/love-that-dare-not-squeak-its-name.html.

p. 144: "When we heard . . . have a child" and "yet another example . . . humans imitating animals": Jennifer 8. Lee, "A Baby for the Gay Authors Behind the Daddy Penguins," *New York Times*, October 2, 2009, https://cityroom.blogs.nytimes .com/2009/10/02/a-baby-for-the-gay-authors-behind-the-daddy-penguins/.

p. 155: "The bottom line . . . life choices": "Librarian: Media Fictionalized *Tango* Penguin Flap," *American Libraries*, Vol. 37, issue 4 (April 2006): 15.

SONYA SONES

p. 159: "card-carrying member . . . since 2004" and "I decided not to . . . my characters":

Sonya Sones, "Getting Banned Part 4: Sonya Sones' Musings of a Sexually Explicit Author," *Los Angeles Review of Books* blog, September 29, 2011, https://tumblr .lareviewofbooks.org/post/24379226314/getting-banned-part-4-sonya-sones-musings -of-a.

R. L. STINE

p. 174: "I work very hard . . . I write about": Mary B. W. Tabor, "At Home With: R. L. Stine; Grown-Ups Deserve Some Terror, Too," *New York Times*, September 7, 1995, C1, https://www.nytimes.com/1995/09/07/garden/at-home-with-r-l-stine-grown-ups -deserve-some-terror-too.html.

ANGIE THOMAS

p. 188: "There are stories . . . through your writing": Deesha Philyaw, "One-on-One with 'The Hate U Give' Novelist Angie Thomas," *Ebony*, March 14, 2017, https://www .ebony.com/entertainment/the-hate-u-give-angie-thomas/.

p. 189: "I was raised knowing . . . way rappers write": Maria Russo, "'I Want to Write the Way Rappers Write': Angie Thomas Discusses the Challenges of Writing Her First Book after 'The Hate U Give,'" *New York Times*, February 1, 2019, C21.

SELECTED READING

MATT DE LA PEÑA

Ball Don't Lie. New York: Delacorte, 2005.

Carmela Full of Wishes. Illustrated by Christian Robinson. New York: Putnam, 2018.

Last Stop on Market Street. Illustrated by Christian Robinson. New York: Putnam, 2015.

Love. Illustrated by Loren Long. New York: Putnam, 2018.

Mexican WhiteBoy. New York: Delacorte, 2008.

We Were Here. New York: Delacorte, 2009.

ROBIE H. HARRIS

Before You Were Three: How You Began to Walk, Talk, Explore, and Have Feelings. Cowritten with Elizabeth Levy, photographs by Henry E. F. Gordillo. New York: Delacorte, 1977.

The Day Leo Said I Hate You! Illustrated by Molly Bang. New York: Little, Brown, 2008.

I Hate Kisses. Illustrated by Diane Paterson. New York: Knopf, 1981.

It's Not the Stork! A Book about Girls, Boys, Babies, Bodies, Families, and Friends. Illustrated by Michael Emberley. Somerville, MA: Candlewick, 2006.

It's Perfectly Normal: Changing Bodies, Growing Up, Sex, and Sexual Health. Illustrated by Michael Emberley. Twentieth anniversary ed. Somerville, MA: Candlewick, 2014.

It's So Amazing! A Book about Eggs, Sperm, Birth, Babies, and Families. Illustrated by Michael Emberley. Fifteenth anniversary ed. Somerville, MA: Candlewick, 2014.

LET'S TALK ABOUT YOU AND ME SERIES:

What's So Yummy? All About Eating Well and Feeling Good. Illustrated by Nadine Bernard Westcott. Somerville, MA: Candlewick, 2014.

What's in There? All About Before You Were Born. Illustrated by Nadine Bernard Westcott. Somerville, MA: Candlewick, 2013.

Who Has What? All About Girls' Bodies and Boys' Bodies. Illustrated by Nadine Bernard Westcott. Somerville, MA: Candlewick, 2011.

Who We Are! All About Being the Same and Being Different. Illustrated by Nadine Bernard Westcott. Somerville, MA: Candlewick, 2016.

Who's in My Family? All About Our Families. Illustrated by Nadine Bernard Westcott. Somerville, MA: Candlewick, 2012.

SUSAN KUKLIN

Beyond Magenta: Transgender Teens Speak Out. Somerville, MA: Candlewick, 2014.

Dance. Cowritten with Bill T. Jones. New York: Hyperion, 1998.

Fighting Back: What Some People Are Doing About AIDS. New York: Putnam, 1989.

In Search of Safety: Voices of Refugees. Somerville, MA: Candlewick, 2020.

Mine for a Year. New York: Coward-McCann/Putnam, 1984.

No Choirboy: Murder, Violence, and Teenagers on Death Row. New York: Henry Holt, 2008.

Thinking Big: The Story of a Young Dwarf. New York: Lothrop, Lee & Shepard, 1986.

Trial: The Inside Story. New York: Henry Holt, 2001.

We Are Here to Stay: Voices of Undocumented Young Adults. Somerville, MA: Candlewick, 2019.

DAVID LEVITHAN

Another Day. New York: Knopf, 2015.

Boy Meets Boy. New York: Knopf, 2003.

Every Day. New York: Knopf, 2012.

Hold Me Closer: The Tiny Cooper Story. New York: Dutton, 2015.

Nick and Norah's Infinite Playlist. Cowritten with Rachel Cohn. New York: Knopf, 2006.

Someday. New York: Knopf, 2018.

Two Boys Kissing. New York: Knopf, 2013.

MEG MEDINA

Burn Baby Burn. Somerville, MA: Candlewick, 2016.

Merci Suárez Changes Gears. Somerville, MA: Candlewick, 2018.

Tía Isa Wants a Car. Illustrated by Claudio Muñoz. Somerville, MA: Candlewick, 2011.

Yaqui Delgado Wants to Kick Your Ass. Somerville, MA: Candlewick, 2013.

LESLÉA NEWMAN

Cats, Cats, Cats! Illustrated by Erika Oller. New York: Simon & Schuster, 2001.

Daddy, Papa, and Me. Illustrated by Carol Thompson. Berkeley, CA: Tricycle, 2009.

Dogs, Dogs, Dogs! Illustrated by Erika Oller. New York: Simon & Schuster, 2002.

A Fire Engine for Ruthie. Illustrated by Cyd Moore. New York: Clarion, 2004.

Hachiko Waits: Based on a True Story. Illustrated by Machiyo Kodaira. New York: Henry Holt, 2004.

Heather Has Two Mommies. Illustrated by Laura Cornell. Somerville, MA: Candlewick, 2015. First published, illustrated by Diane Souza, 1989 by Other World Publishing, 1990 by Alyson Books.

Ketzel, the Cat Who Composed. Illustrated by Amy June Bates. Somerville, MA: Candlewick, 2015.

Mommy, Mama, and Me. Illustrated by Carol Thompson. Berkeley, CA: Tricycle, 2009.

October Mourning: A Song for Matthew Shepard. Somerville, MA: Candlewick, 2012.

Sparkle Boy. Illustrated by Maria Mola. New York: Lee & Low, 2017.

KATHERINE PATERSON

Bridge to Terabithia. Illustrated by Donna Diamond. New York: Crowell, 1977.

The Great Gilly Hopkins. New York: Crowell, 1978.

Jacob Have I Loved. New York: Crowell, 1980.

Jip: His Story. New York: Lodestar, 1996.

The Master Puppeteer. Illustrated by Haru Wells. New York: Crowell, 1975.

Park's Quest. New York: Lodestar, 1988.

Preacher's Boy. New York: Clarion, 1999.

The Sign of the Chrysanthemum. Illustrated by Peter Landa. New York: Crowell, 1977.

DAV PILKEY

Big Dog and Little Dog series. New York: Houghton Mifflin Harcourt, 1997–1999.

Captain Underpants series. New York: Scholastic, 1997–.

Dog Man series. New York: Scholastic, 2016–.

Dumb Bunnies series. New York: Scholastic, 1994–1997.

Ricky Ricotta's Mighty Robot series. New York: Scholastic, 2000–.

World War Won. Kansas City, MO: Landmark, 1987.

JUSTIN RICHARDSON AND PETER PARNELL

And Tango Makes Three. Illustrated by Henry Cole. New York: Simon & Schuster, 2005.

Christian, the Hugging Lion. Illustrated by Amy June Bates. New York: Simon & Schuster, 2010.

JUSTIN RICHARDSON AND MARK A. SCHUSTER

Everything You Never Wanted Your Kids to Know about Sex (But Were Afraid They'd Ask). New York: Crown, 2003.

SONYA SONES

One of Those Hideous Books Where the Mother Dies. New York: Simon & Schuster, 2004.

The Opposite of Innocent. New York: HarperCollins, 2018.

Stop Pretending: What Happened When My Big Sister Went Crazy. New York: HarperCollins, 1999.

What My Girlfriend Doesn't Know. New York: Simon & Schuster, 2007.

What My Mother Doesn't Know. New York: Simon & Schuster, 2001.

R. L. STINE

Blind Date. New York: Scholastic, 1986.

Fear Street series. New York: Scholastic, 1989–.

Goosebumps series. New York: Scholastic, 1992–.

ANGIE THOMAS

The Hate U Give. New York: Balzer + Bray, 2017.

On the Come Up. New York: Balzer + Bray, 2019.

INDEX